IMPROBABLY SUCCESSFUL

Proven Career Growth Strategies for the Rest of Us

JUAN SILVERA

ISBN 979-8-9909702-0-5 (softcover)
ISBN 979-8-9909702-1-2 (ebook)
ISBN 979-8-9909702-2-9 (PDF)

The advice and strategies contained herein may not be suitable
for your situation. You should consult with a professional when
appropriate. Neither the publisher nor the author shall be liable for
any loss of income or any other damages, including but not limited
to special, incidental, consequential, personal, or other damages.

For privacy reasons, some names, locations, and
dates may have been changed.

Editing: Stacey Miller
Cover design, interior design, and book layout:
KUHN Design Group | kuhndesigngroup.com

SIGO LLC
Charlotte, NC
United States of America

To connect with the author or for business inquiries:
https://linktr.ee/juansilvera

"A valuable collection of insightful and actionable advice. *Improbably Successful* masterfully distills complex career concepts into accessible, relatable guidance that resonates deeply with professionals at all stages. Whether you're just starting out, seeking to make a significant career pivot, or aiming to climb the corporate ladder, this book offers a fresh perspective on achieving success. Its emphasis on leveraging one's unique background and experiences as strengths is particularly empowering."

Fernanda Leal-Pardinas, MD, MSc
Executive Medical Director, Clinical Development
Sarepta Therapeutics

"In *Improbably Successful*, Juan Silvera offers poignant, practical, firsthand knowledge of career growth strategies for those that don't necessarily match the stereotypical corporate professional. His pragmatism, dry wit, and no bull approach makes this guide a pleasure to read and easy to implement."

Vickie Sherman
Chief Marketing Officer
Pacific Premier Bank

"*Improbably Successful* offers invaluable insights and practical advice for navigating the complexities of career development. Its unique approach demystifies career advancement strategies, making it an essential read for individuals at any stage of their professional journey."

Faisal Sheikh
Former Executive Director Human Resources
Rabobank North America

To my wife Angela and her unconditional support of my improbable career and to our amazing daughters, Andrea and Vanessa, for making me a better person. I love you!

.

CONTENTS

INTRODUCTION

When you think of a successful corporate career, you would never think that it could start in the infamous Comuna 13 neighborhood in Medellin, Colombia. But that is where mine began. Despite the amazing transformation that Medellin has undergone in the last few years, the city was rough long before Hollywood began romanticizing Pablo, Griselda, and other local bad apples.

One of my very earliest memories as a child back in Medellin was looking out my window and seeing a street knife fight between two teenage boys that resulted in one of them going home to God and the other one following him shortly thereafter. Sometimes, things like that just happened in my neighborhood. But rather than traumatizing us kids, those events developed in us a sense for survival and an almost infallible "friend or foe radar" that would come in very handy in the business world decades later.

But the truth is that, in today's hypercompetitive global job market, the best survival instincts earned on the mean streets, or even the best planned career path, coupled with a great formal education, are simply not enough to get ahead. And if you happen to be a woman or a person of color in the U.S. or anywhere in the West for that matter, it is even tougher. The good news is that there is a set of proven career management strategies and best practices that, when used deliberately and consistently, can propel your career. The other good news is that, perhaps surprisingly, being a woman or a person of color can actually work to your advantage under certain circumstances when those things that are part of who you are match traits that lead to professional success. And that is what this book is about. It is a guide for career success for those who may not fit the stereotypical profile of a senior executive. It is a practical career management guide for the rest of us.

The motivation for writing this book is simple: Professionals in my network often reach out to me when they are just starting their professional lives, when they are looking for a new job, or when they want to advance in their current job. They look at my work trajectory and figure that I must have done something right. I'm always happy to oblige, because nearly everyone who has had any kind of successful career has received help from others somewhere along the way. Unless you are born into immense privilege, somebody, some time, probably has lent you a hand. So I'm always happy to help in any way I can.

The problem, of course, is that one-on-one, personalized mentorship simply does not scale. So the idea is to capture in this book what I have learned over many years and share that with whomever can use sound, practical, real-life career advice.

So who exactly can benefit from this book? Although the strategies captured here may resonate more with those who are not the typical professionals found in executive management and boardrooms, the fact is anybody who wants to grow professionally can benefit from the ideas captured here. Whether you are a recent college graduate, a mid-career professional looking for the next step upward, or a more seasoned pro looking to finally break through the C-suite, there's something here for you. Best of all, everything you read here is based on real-life experiences, not theory or academic work.

We start by exploring the topic of long-term goal setting, which is quite possibly the most important part of your journey. That will lead us into understanding the concept of career non-linearity, which is an exploration of the fact that professional progression is rarely a nice, straight, upward path. Part of that not-so-straight road may require you to be flexible in terms of location, so we will explore that concept at length here. By the way, you will see that this approach to building your career is every bit as valid today, when remote work has become more common.

We will then look at networking from a new angle. All career coaches underscore the importance of networking, but there are sub-tleties and approaches to optimize the time you invest in network-ing, and I will share them here. The book also goes deep into the critical topic of how to best manage your professional brand. This is an area that many high-potential professionals neglect, and it is rel-atively easy to manage. When it comes to your career, your image is paramount, and this book will cover specific tactics to help you mar-ket yourself professionally and effectively.

While all these dimensions of managing one's career are critical, my real-life experience has taught me that there is one skill that has the greatest positive impact in your professional progression, and that is Communication. That's right, Communication with a capital C. The good news is that you don't need to be a natural-born TED speaker to advance your career through effective communication. I will share with you proven communications strategies that will set you apart, even from those that have the gift of great oratory.

We then get to the crux of the matter, and that is how a person like you or me, who may not necessarily fit the stereotypical profile of a successful executive (at least by Western standards) can use our uniqueness to win in the marketplace. The epiphany that brought me here is that what is normally considered a set of inherent disadvantages in the workplace for women and folks of color, turn out to be a professional's greatest competitive advantage. In fact, that is one of the primary motivators that drove me to write this book. I want to share with you real-life strategies and tactics to turn who you are at your core into career success. It has worked for me, and I want it to work for you.

The book ends with the power of sharing what you learn here with others who are also looking to move ahead professionally. Turns out that selfless mentorship and sharing what you've learned over your career is not just great, altruistic work, although it is that. Sometimes, it also comes back to help YOU.

The book also includes a collection of "Improbable Facts" featuring data points and insights that you may want to take note of as you go. Think of these little "nuggets" as shortcuts to help you get to a key point quicker.

CHAPTER 1

STARTING WITH THE END

Every great endeavor starts with a vision of some kind. And a great career is no exception. However, there's no one-size-fits-all vision, because we all want different things. Sure, there is this universal wish for the perfect life, with a perfect job and the perfect family. But the specifics are different for everyone. The fact is that achieving such a utopia is rare, and for many, it does not define success. Every journey is different, and our aspirations are, and should be, our own. Still, you need a plan and a vision. Without them, you are likely to flounder from job to job, waiting for a stroke of luck or some revelation that will change the course of your life.

The thing is that, for some, especially when we are young and starting our careers, it is difficult to envision that ideal future. Sometimes, we are just not sure what we want to do. Over the years, I have mentored people with this predicament, and what I always ask them is this: Forget about a professional career. What do you really enjoy doing? Never mind what society defines as a successful professional. What do you really, really like to do? Sometimes, the answer is, "I like to listen to music." Or, "I really like watching sports on TV" or playing video games. Rarely is the answer something like, "I love corporate litigation." Or, "I really love compliance and regulatory work in the banking industry." But, in fact, no matter what you really love, there is a good chance that, with a good plan and perseverance, you can make a living doing just that.

IMPROBABLE FACT #1

Today, there are professional gamers who make hundreds of thousands, or even millions, of dollars a year. Professional surfers, skate boarders, musicians, athletes, travel vloggers… they all make a living doing what they love. So while it is true that, in some of these fields, natural talent is required, often it is a solid plan and a vision that allow these individuals to fulfill their professional dreams.

A few years back, I took a job in the San Francisco Bay area, and my family moved to a town in Marin County, just on the other side of the Golden Gate Bridge. By incredible coincidence, our neighbor across the street was Lars Ulrich, drummer for Metallica. His father, the great Torben Ulrich, and his wife, Molly, lived in a home next to us. My wife and I developed a very nice friendship with Torben and Molly. Sometimes, we would have them over to our home, and they sometimes would have us over to theirs. Those were great dinner parties, because Torben and Molly had the best stories from the worlds of professional sports (Torben was a world class-tennis player) and rock 'n' roll. Torben shared with us that his family moved to Southern

California when Lars was a teenager, because he wanted to play on a high school tennis team with a friend whose father was a player from Torben's generation and a good friend. Rather than pursuing tennis, Lars of course fell in love with music and followed his passion for the drums, co-founded Metallica, and the rest is, well, rock 'n' roll history. He had a plan and a vision, and he knew what he wanted.

In my particular case, as a child, I loved telling stories and having an audience that I could persuade to do this and that. I loved marketing; I just didn't know that such a thing existed until late in high school and early in college. But once I realized that I could make a living telling stories and convincing others to do something, then I knew that was what I wanted to do.

After that came the realization that, at a certain level, you could make a nice living in marketing, especially at the top of the profession (for example, as a chief marketing officer in a large organization). It was at that moment that I built a plan to get there. I had a plan and a vision, and I knew what I wanted.

Naturally, our vision and aspirations have to live within reality. At 5 feet and 7 inches tall and of average athleticism, the mathematical probabilities of my playing professional basketball were, well, near zero. So my best plans and vision to play in the NBA would be more than improbable. But, for any professional endeavor that involved using my brain and my words, the sky was probably the limit.

THE LONG HAUL

When it comes to a well-managed career, persistence and perseverance can be your best friends. Sure, there are entrepreneurs who quit Harvard, start a tech company, and are billionaires by age twenty-five. But believe me that these are outliers, true exceptions. That is why they are famous, and you know who they are. For the rest of us, however, there is typically a multi-year journey to the top of our professions.

The English word "career" dates back to the mid-sixteenth century (denoting a road or racecourse). It comes from the French carrière, which is from the Italian carriera, based on the Latin carrus "wheeled vehicle." The concept of a career denotes a race, a journey. In fact, in the Spanish language, career translates to "carrera," which is the same word (spelling and all) used for race. The concept is really more akin to a marathon than, say, a 100-yard dash.

Linguistics notwithstanding, it is important we understand that a great career usually takes time. That is not to say, however, that we should passively wait decades until we reach our destination based on perseverance. Quite the opposite; a well-managed career is a deliberate, well-planned, and smartly executed process. It's not an overnight thing.

That does not mean that we advance in our careers by simply putting in the time. Time alone will not give you the kind of sustained, upwardly mobile career progression that you want. In fact, a phenomenon I have observed is that, sometimes, professionals who stay for many years in a single role are not considered for jobs at a new company. This is because prospective employers perceive this kind of "stability" as stagnation or, worse, lack of ambition and inertia. This, of course, is a paradox. On the one hand, employers want you to hang around for a while, but when a person does so, in the eyes of another company, the candidate can get the dreaded "lifer" tag.

Naturally, there is nothing wrong with finding a job you really like and staying put for years, perfectly content with your work, your compensation, and your level. One of my best friends from college landed a role as a first responder in California and worked there, in more or less the same capacity, until retirement. That was his personal choice, and there is nothing wrong with it. If that is you, this book is probably not for you.

If you want to grow professionally over time, though—unless you are some type of prodigy—you should understand that the bigger, best remunerated roles take some time to achieve. Unless, of course, you follow the entrepreneurial path.

So why, exactly, does it often take decades to get to the C-suite or a role of an equivalent level? For one thing, some of the skills necessary to hold those roles require the type of experience and maturity that only time can teach. For example, in the course of a day, a seasoned manager can make dozens of decisions, from the mundane to the strategic. Great managers will make decisions quickly, and the overwhelming percentage of them will be considered "good decisions." The reason these effective leaders can do that is because their brains hold a huge database of past experiences that inform fast, mostly wise, decision-making. The brightest twenty-three-year-old just does not have that body of references yet. It takes time to build that kind of mental "library."

The other reason success, more times than not, takes a while is because so much of it depends on a sizable, vibrant professional network. And that takes time to build. Back in the 2010s, when I was head of digital marketing for a large bank in San Francisco, LinkedIn invited me to their offices and gave me a personalized infographic that showed highlights of my LinkedIn account. It showed that my very first connection was Edy Weber, who was the head of technology at ElSitio.com, a first-generation consumer web portal from Argentina. Edy and I connected on LinkedIn in June 2004, when LinkedIn had fewer than 800,000 members. I met Edy in the late nineties, during the dot com boom. Since then, my professional network has continued to grow. Today, if I need a job lead from a top-notch IT leader in Argentina, I know who to reach out to. The same would be true if I need one in California, Netherlands, North Carolina, or Austria. But it's taken more than three decades to build that amazing network. More on networking later in the book.

SETTING YOUR JOB TENURE CYCLE

Now that we've established that it takes a bit of time to get ahead, the question is: Can you do this while staying long term at the same organization, or is there an ideal job tenure cycle? The answer is, of course, it depends on your definition of success and the value you place on stability.

For example, if your goal is early retirement, even if it means living more modestly after you retire, then a career in public service, government, or the military is probably a good path for you. Some jobs in these areas still come with some type of pension and other compelling retirement benefits, but you may have to stay put in a single place, doing pretty much the same kind of work, for decades. One of my best friends from college did just that. He graduated and went to work as an IT systems analyst with the city of Los Angeles, and he stayed there until he retired in his mid-fifties. His wife also worked in technology for the city, so now they enjoy a comfortable retired life in a suburb in L.A.

Nothing wrong with this strategy. It is a safe, pragmatic path. But what is also true is that with this stability comes an opportunity cost. By that I mean: You give up all of the learning opportunities, income upside, and life experiences that come from changing jobs every now and then, and from the occasional move around the world.

For those who are more adventurous and further out in the risk/reward curve, what is the right job tenure strategy and cycle? A 2022 study conducted by the Pew Institute revealed that the typical American who changed employers in the year from April 2021 to March 2022 got a 9.7% bump in their "real" wages compared to a year earlier. This period of time, of course, was around the time of the COVID pandemic, which was characterized by high demand for workers of all types. This, in turn, resulted in wage inflation. The same study pointed out that workers who switched jobs did better than those who stayed put. The median worker who remained at the same job from April 2021 to March 2022 saw their earnings fall by 1.7% after accounting for inflation, according to the study.

This data is consistent with my own experience and what I have observed over the last thirty-plus years. You don't have to be a math genius to figure that, over a multi-decade career, the "compounding" effect of these self-awarded raises can add up to hundreds of thousands of dollars. Pretend that you stay in the same place for thirty years, earning an average annual merit salary increase of 3%. Now imagine that, every four to five years, you change jobs, and every time you do so, you pick up a bump of 15% to 20% (which is not unreasonable if you market yourself right), plus perhaps a sign-on bonus. Over the course of time, the latter strategy translates into much higher wages.

The following table contrasts the earnings of an individual who starts a job earning $100,000 per year and stays with the same company earning an average annual merit increase of 3% versus another one who changes jobs every three years and, in doing so, picks up an incremental 20% increase every time. The analysis, which assumes a twenty-year career, shows a difference of more than $1,300,000 in earnings over that time.

Starting Salary	Yr 1	Yr 4	Yr 8	Yr 12	Yr 16	Yr 20	Total
$100,000	$100,000	$103,000	$106,090	$109,273	$112,551	$115,927	$2,687,037
$100,000	$100,000	$120,000	$144,000	$172,800	$207,360	$248,832	$4,033,109

As shocking as the difference in the two numbers may be, it only tells part of the story. It does not reflect the impact of things like larger employer 401k contributions resulting from greater earnings. It also should be pointed out that the same "multiplier" effect can be achieved if you are promoted within the same company and those promotions come with increases commensurate with those you would have obtained when you changed jobs.

The trick, though, is to find a balance between being a lifer and changing jobs so often that prospective employers perceive that you cannot hold onto a job. After all, job instability is one of the major red flags that recruiters and hiring managers pick up when considering candidates. During my career, which spans three plus decades as a marketing and banking executive around the world, I have hired or supervised hiring managers who have evaluated hundreds of job candidates, and one of the most frequent early disqualifiers has been short job tenure.

Unless there is a very compelling explanation, a candidate with a string of jobs with two or fewer years in tenure projects instability, incompetence, or both. There are some exceptions to this phenomenon, and one of them applies to early career candidates. When I worked for a top four bank in Charlotte, NC, I was hiring a digital marketing specialist and came across the résumé of a person who had all the right credentials, had experience with the right marketing tech tools, and graduated from a very reputable school. Her résumé, however, showed three jobs over the last three years. I was ready to toss her résumé aside, but then I looked at her college graduation date and realized that she had graduated just four years ago. One more look at the résumé showed me increasing levels of responsibility over the three years. Bottom line: She was a very strong candidate and was simply progressing rapidly as she outgrew initial entry-level jobs. After a great job interview, I hired her. I still have her as a contact on LinkedIn. She has done amazingly well for herself changing jobs, on average, every four to five years.

CHAPTER 2

THE NON-LINEAR
CAREER PATH

When I was a principal at my first digital marketing agency start-up in the mid-nineties, one of the firm's partners often bragged about how smart his son was and how dad knew already that his kid had the caliber to become president of the United States. He made statements like these very seriously and, of course, those around him took it all with a grain of salt.

Now, as of the writing of this book, my friend's son has not yet moved into the White House. But he did turn out to be an exceptional scholar, earning a Ph.D. in brain and cognitive sciences from MIT and completing his postdoctoral studies at Stanford. He was also a Marshall Scholar at Oxford, studying linguistics, after completing his undergraduate degree in English from Harvard. Today, he enjoys a successful career in academia and is a Google Research Scholar.

People like this actually exist and their talent, coupled with the opportunities that life affords them, often enjoy a nice, "linear" career path. For some, it all starts with an exceptional formal education, followed by a meaningful internship, all leading to a prestigious, lucrative career. The thing is, this is not normal—at least, not for the rest of us. More than likely, professional success follows a non-linear path in which, sometimes, you take two steps forward and one step back.

If you were to plot the successful careers of those of us who do not start with everything in our favor, it would probably look like the U.S. stock market over the last hundred years. Overall, it trends upwards, but with dips and setbacks along the way. This table illustrates this pattern (over a thirty-year career), assigning a hypothetical success factor that could be compensation, job fulfillment, or any other such measurement of your choice.

THE TYPICAL NON-LINEAR SUCCESSFUL CAREER

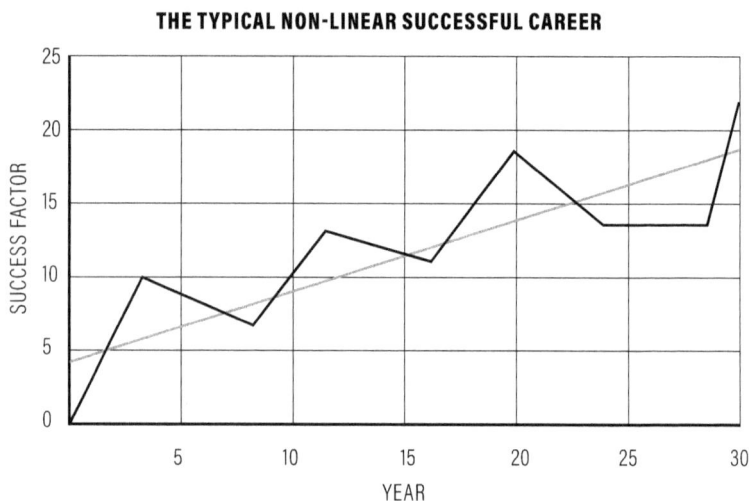

So now that we understand that a professional career normally does not follow a smooth, consistent upward trend, what strategies can we leverage to ensure that, setbacks notwithstanding, we win over the course of time?

EARLY CAREER "INVESTMENTS"

The first one is the concept of what I call "early career investments." By that, I mean those things you do that represent some short-term sacrifice but that pave the way for professional success down the road. In my case, one such investment came as I was finishing my MBA at Pepperdine University while working full-time as an analyst at Dun & Bradstreet in Los Angeles. As prestigious as being an analyst with D&B sounded, that role was very much an entry-level opportunity performing repetitive tasks. My plan was simply to complete my degree and look for a more meaningful, better paying job, commensurate with my newly earned MBA degree.

But just as I was planning my next move, my manager at Dun & Bradstreet asked me if I would consider a six-month assignment at the company's Mexico City offices. The assignment consisted of preparing and delivering a training program for analysts throughout Latin America. This sounded like a great opportunity to gain international exposure and experience the "expat life." The bad news? There would be no increase in pay, and accommodations in Mexico City would be substandard. However, after discussing the opportunity with my wife, Angela, I decided to go for it. The thinking was simply that, even if in the short-term I would be leaving some money on the table, the opportunity to work internationally, even if it was only for six months, would be a great résumé builder and set me up for future, more meaningful opportunities. So together, we decided that this was a worthwhile investment and, within a few days of graduation, we packed our things and drove from L.A. to Mexico City for our new adventure.

As it turns out, the investment paid dividends relatively quickly. One of the D&B offices that I had to visit to train the trainers was in Caracas, Venezuela. During my stay, I was approached by the company's country manager about taking over the operations manager role, overseeing a team of about thirty people, mostly located in Caracas. The pay was better, but most importantly, living conditions were great, and I learned a ton about managing people in another country. We moved to Venezuela and stayed on the role until D&B decided to close its offices there as a result of a deteriorating business environment. And so, even though that assignment lasted only a year, when combined with my half a year in Mexico and my newly minted MBA, it gave me a very interesting professional profile before I turned thirty.

But none of this would have happened if I hadn't made the decision to give up short-term rewards in exchange for making an investment in the future. So, as you set your own career path, it would be wise to always consider professional opportunities that, on the surface, may not appear to follow a nice linear path to success. Consider how the opportunity would shape your professional profile and how it might set you apart from the competition. Rewards will surely come later as you gain experience and develop a competitive advantage in the job market.

Incidentally, the Mexico City opportunity was offered to me because I was the only Spanish-speaking analyst in the L.A. office at that time. Remember this fact later on as we get into the topic of using your differences to your advantage.

THE POWER OF THE LATERAL MOVE

A well-planned lateral move is another strategy that at first may seem counterintuitive but often works. A lateral move is a career move whereby you take on a different role at a similar level to that which you currently have. Now, you may ask: Why would I want to make a move to do something where I make the same amount of money (or maybe even a bit less)? The answer is because a lateral move can help you get closer to your next move up. Suppose, for example, that you work at a bank and you are motivated by money. Yes, you like nice corporate titles and recognition, but what really drives you is compensation. You are currently a project manager somewhere in the operations department of the company. It is a nice job, but without a lot of room for income growth. Every year, you are awarded a marginal merit salary increase that, in most years is at par with inflation, and perhaps a small bonus, if you perform well and the company meets its goals.

Now, one day, you hear that the folks in the bank's investment banking division make a ton of money—specifically, if they are client-facing and making deals. In addition to your project management skills, you also sell yourself well and are very persistent. The problem is, the investment banking folks won't consider you because, even though you know financial services, they prefer to hire people with experience in their specific area. It would seem that door is closed, until one day you learn that there is a project manager role in the investment banking business, and you certainly qualify for the job. The pay, grade, and title are nearly the same as that of your current role, but making this lateral move places you inside the investment banking team. From there, you can gradually learn that part of the business, get a mentor, and request that, as part of your development plan, you have the chance to shadow the sales team. After that, you are well-positioned for a junior role in the sales team, learning how to make deals from the best. You are now well on your way to becoming an investment banker…and the potential for earning the great income that comes with that.

Naturally, this plan may take you a few years to execute, and there are no guarantees that it will work. However, your downside is minimal. Even if you didn't eventually land a role with better compensation, you were still a project manager during that time, never making less than when you were in the operations department.

The lateral move strategy can also be used when you want to join a specific company, which sometimes may mean making some short-term sacrifices to reach your ultimate goal. I saw this firsthand when a friend of mine who was a recruiter in the Bay Area for a private mid-market recruiting firm specializing in tech roles told me that her dream was to get into a big tech company in Silicon Valley. She had friends who worked there and were doing quite well between salary, bonus and, in some cases, stock options or grants. Based on all of this, and because she loved the Google brand, she set her sights on working for Alphabet, Google's parent company. She learned through a friend that there was an associate level recruiting role that had just opened at her target company, and she applied.

During the interview process she was disappointed to learn that the role paid approximately 10% less than what she was making at that time. However, she also learned that the recruiting job family at Alphabet had very senior roles with interesting income potential and upside. So she took the job and the short term pay cut, but there she was, working at her dream company and with tons of room to grow. A few years after her move I learned, through LinkedIn, that she had gotten a promotion, the second one in less than four years. She was well on her way, thanks to the power of the lateral move!

THE BIG FISH IN A LITTLE POND

A similar strategy, and just as effective, is what I call the *big fish in the small pond* move. This career management technique involves placing oneself in an important role, with an impressive corporate or functional title, at a smaller organization as a stepping stone leading to a similar role at a larger company.

This approach works because, for large roles (with meaningful compensation packages), recruiters and hiring managers often look for candidates who have done a similar job at another place. For example, a large enterprise looking for a chief information officer will normally give greater consideration to a candidate who has been a CIO somewhere else. In our example, and everything else being the same, a candidate with a CIO title on their current role at a smaller company will be given more consideration than a senior technology manager at another large organization, even if that candidate had a significantly higher level of responsibility.

The reason this happens is partly due to optics. Highly visible jobs, like those with a "C" in their title, often call for somebody with the credentials and pedigree required for the role. In other words, it is easier to "sell" internally a candidate who has done the job already (even if was at a smaller scale). All this means that, as a professional, you may consider taking a job with less responsibility (and perhaps a bit less compensation) with a bigger title to get into the "executive club."

Let's say, for example, that your long-term goal is to be the chief financial officer at a Fortune 500 company. You know you have the knowledge and capacity for such a role. But how do you even become part of the consideration set for a role like that? The answer may well be to find a way to land that first job as a CFO at a mid-size or rapidly growing, well positioned smaller company. You may have to take a couple of these jobs, and you will still need to compete with seasoned CFOs for your dream role, but now you will be given consideration. You are one step closer to the big time.

This is a strategy I applied in my own case. Like any marketer with ambitions, I always wanted the "top job." I wanted to be a CMO. Having worked under CMOs earlier in my career, I had come to the conclusion that as brilliant as these executives were, they were not doing anything that I could not do. I knew I was ready but needed to take the jump. At that time, I was the head of digital marketing for Union Bank, a large regional bank based in California which was a wholly owned subsidiary of MUFG, a gigantic Japanese global bank. The company, the role, and my peers were all great, but after many years of specializing exclusively in digital marketing, I was concerned that, if I stayed in digital much longer, it would be hard to land a CMO role.

I also knew, however, that it would be hard to go from being a head of digital marketing at a super-regional bank to being CMO at a top twenty bank. So the answer was to look for, and find, a smaller company that needed a CMO with extensive digital experience. I tapped into my extensive professional network, and one of my old college friends tipped me off that his employer, Rabobank N.A, was looking for a new CMO.

At that time, Rabobank N.A. (a subsidiary of Dutch banking giant Rabobank) was much smaller than Union Bank, which meant it had smaller budgets and resources, and that also meant I'd take a small pay cut for going there.

As soon as I heard about the Rabobank role opening, I reached out directly to their CEO and, within days, I had an interview and was offered the job. After two decades in the marketing field, I was finally a CMO! The budget and team size for that role were not particularly large, and the job didn't even report directly to the CEO, but it was a "C" job at a subsidiary of a very large global company. I was a big fish in a little pond and my résumé had just gotten a huge upgrade.

CHAPTER 3

MOBILITY

Whenever I travel for work to places where I have lived before, I love calling old friends and business acquaintances to see if they are willing to meet. This practice is tons of fun, as you get to reminisce. It is also a great way to keep your professional network alive and relevant.

One thing that strikes me whenever I do this is that the vast majority of these connections still live (and sometimes work) in the same place where I originally met them. I suppose this is normal, since most people have roots at home. Their parents live there; their spouses or partners may have careers there; or maybe they just love where they live as a place to raise a family.

I have to confess that there are times when I wish our family would have stayed put in one place for at least ten years. There's something to be said for stability and the comfort of familiar surroundings.

However, looking at it strictly from a career management point of view, the benefits of mobility and what I call "the big move" are undeniable. Today, we live in a global labor market. In my parents' generation, the place where you were born and raised was also your job marketplace. Lost your job? Pick up the local newspaper and see who is hiring in town. It's clear that has not been the case for a long time, and now employers will look everywhere for the right person.

Naturally, the emergence of telecommuting, which accelerated dramatically during the COVID-19 pandemic, means that you can stay in your hometown and have a very nice job anywhere in the world without leaving home. However, most career development experts and executives agree that nothing replaces being on-site, at the office (preferably at the company's headquarters), if you want exposure and advancement.

Therefore, ambitious professionals should always consider relocation, under the right circumstances, and for the right opportunity. The benefits of a big move (where you go to another part of the world to take a job) go well beyond the professional advantages.

Every city, country, and company have their own unique cultures and idiosyncrasies, and very few things can enrich your life as much as immersing yourself in something new and different. I have also learned that working in different places makes you a better manager, because you learn to work with people with every imaginable communication and work style. Each of those work experiences are stored in your brain and become part of your leadership playbook, to be used in the future.

IMPROBABLE FACT #2

A big move transforms your professional profile by showing you as a well-rounded professional who is in demand to the point where companies are willing to move you so that you can take on a job. This is even truer if at least one of the big moves involves an international assignment. International work experience positions you at another level of professionalism and separates you from the competition.

A big move also signals to future potential employers that you are adaptable and that you can take calculated risks for the right reason. These are all very desirable traits in any professional. If you're a young professional starting your career, an international assignment, even if it isn't for a dream job, can position you for success and positive differentiation down the road. In my case, for example, having two jobs outside of the U.S. by my early thirties helped me position myself as an "international" candidate, and that proved to be invaluable in subsequent years.

WHEN BIG MOVES MAKE SENSE

However, a big move is not for everybody. So when does it make sense to make such a move? Under what set of circumstances should you move for your next assignment? Here's a checklist:

1. The move represents real career progression. If you are offered a role across the country or across the world with

the same level of responsibility and compensation, and with a company more or less as prestigious as your current one, then such a move probably does not make sense. The exception, of course, would be if you are attracted to the location of the new job for quality-of-life reasons. Example: You are an associate analyst in the heart of the U.S. Midwest, and you hate winter. If there is an opportunity for the same job in Hawaii, you probably should consider it. Otherwise, you will want to see an improvement over your current status or pay to compensate for the inconvenience and uncertainty of a big move. With an out-of-town move, you should be looking at more money, a better title, greater responsibility, a more prestigious employer, or a combination of all of these.

2. The move does not represent a significant financial setback for you. Earlier in the book, we talked about certain "investments" in your career, but moving yourself at your expense should not be one of them. In my career, I have observed that every big move worth making involves a role in which your new employer will pay for your move. Moves, especially those for professionals with a family, are complicated, disruptive, and very expensive. You should not subsidize a large company, even if it is for your dream job. Also, please remember that even the best relocation package will not cover certain expenses involved with your move. While a company may pay for your move, transportation of your car, and the cost of selling and buying your old and new homes, they will not cover that one new sofa that you are going to need for your new home. That is the reason you

should also always negotiate some type of sign-on bonus, to cover those things that the relocation package will not.

3. The move is a win on the personal front. A big move must also be a positive for your family, if you have one. That means that your spouse or partner and your children, if you have any, must also benefit in some fashion from the change. I know former colleagues with spouses who sacrificed their jobs for the more lucrative out-of-town job only to come to regret the decision when the spouse or partner could not find an equivalent job at the new location. Worse, while the new job holder loved the new role, the rest of the family hated their new surroundings or got homesick.

BIG MOVES THAT MAKE SENSE!

Career Progression ✓

No Financial Setback ✓

Personal/Family Win ✓

INTERNATIONAL ASSIGNMENTS

My first "big move" opportunity came to me in the late nineties, a few years after I joined an internet professional services start-up (it was really a digital marketing agency before they started calling them that). The firm had done well for itself, going from three employees to over a hundred full-time colleagues with offices in Florida, Atlanta, and New York City.

It was an exciting time, as we were part of the birth of a new industry. We had an amazing client roster that included the state of Florida (Jeb Bush once visited our offices for the launch of the first-ever Florida.gov site) and Credit Swiss First Boston and Frank Quattrone, who paid us one million dollars for developing their new site, an exorbitant amount for that time.

And then the dot-com bubble burst … fortunately for me, we had hired a brand pro who had an extensive network in marketing in the UK, Germany, and his native Austria. Before things started to go south for the whole internet industry in the U.S., the partners at our agency identified Europe as a potential expansion market. I was paired up with my new Austrian friend to travel to Europe looking for potential acquisition targets, joint ventures, or partnerships.

We visited with agencies in London, Frankfurt, Vienna, and Salzburg. And, in each of these markets, there was a lot of interest in what we were doing, because American digital marketing firms were viewed as being at the cutting edge. The agencies we visited had great client rosters who were eager to go online but, since it was a relatively new space, there just wasn't a lot of local expertise. This all meant that there was a lot of pent-up demand for digital marketing services and, thus, a great business opportunity.

We returned to America very enthused about the possibilities. Unfortunately, this was all occurring at the precise moment when the internet bubble began to burst, and our firm began to lose steam. This meant our plans for European expansion were on hold for good. However, one of the contacts we made, an agency called GGK Salzburg, developed an interest in doing something, anyway, and reached out to me to gauge my appetite for starting a new digital agency to serve big-brand clients they had in Austria and the German-speaking parts of Italy.

The agency had clients eager to get going online, but the expertise was needed. My wife and I flew to Salzburg and stopped in Venice for some time off where the GGK Salzburg managing partner met us. Over dinner and a bottle of wine, we made a deal that would have me move, with my family, to Salzburg to start a new digital marketing agency.

Now, all this sounds very cool now. At the time, though, it was the craziest and most terrifying thing we could have done. This move involved selling our little house in tropical South Florida and moving, along with our three-year-old twin girls, to Salzburg. We spoke no German, had no idea what a winter in the Alps was like, and had very few guarantees for a financial safety net in the event the experiment failed. But we did it, anyway, and off to Austria we went to do a startup!

As scary and risky as the whole venture was, it was also the most exciting thing that I have ever done professionally. Imagine starting a company from zero, with near-complete creative freedom, and in a market with clients who were eagerly wanting help with their digital strategies.

So much (good and not-so-good) happened during our time in Austria that it can be the subject of another book, but, as it pertains to career development, it was one of the most impactful events in my life. During that time, I learned the real meaning of P&L (profit and loss) responsibility, talent acquisition and management, business and market development, and navigating day-to-day company operations (in a language that was not my own).

All of these learnings have been foundational for me, and I still apply them in my professional life today. I was also rewarded richly on the personal front as well since, at the time we started the agency, I was paired up with a young man by the name of Alex Walterskirchen, who went on to co-found Pixelart, one of the largest and most important digital marketing agencies in Austria today. To this day, Alex and I still meet and maintain a friendship that now spans decades.

Two different offshoots of our original agency (which we called Connetation) are still around today. Even though, at one point, our family eventually had to return to the U.S., our "big move" continues to yield rewards to this day. I imagine not every such big move pays off the way mine did, but even if the business reason that prompts such a move does not crystalize, the experience and professional development gained by it often makes it all worth it.

CHAPTER 4

NETWORKING DONE RIGHT

Dozens of books, podcasts, and TED talks are produced and delivered every year on the topic of professional networking. Most of them are invaluable and are predicated on the indisputable fact that, as far as career management goes, networking is a proven winning strategy. Rather than regurgitating what has already been written and spoken about on the topic of networking, I want to provide you some different angles—and strategies—related to professional networking.

SELECTIVE NETWORKING

It has been my experience that not all networking is the same. If your professional aspirations involve, for example, an executive role at a multinational corporation, then the local chamber of commerce mixer is probably not the best networking opportunity. Yes, you will meet great people at such an event, they just won't be the right people to help you achieve your career goals.

A much better approach is to be selective and strategically identify the professional (or maybe even social) circles where people who can open doors for you spend time. The challenge, of course, is that everybody wants access to the same power players, CEOs, and industry movers and shakers that you do. And those folks are constantly besieged by aspiring professionals who want to get on their radar.

However, here's an instance where your uniqueness can work in your favor. If you are, say, a high-potential Black professional who wants to get access to top executives who can open doors, you are more likely to gain access to such leaders if they themselves are Black. Why? Because out of all the people who are looking to get face time with those leaders, you will be one who, in many cases, will likely get special consideration. This is because it is probable that the executive himself was also mentored by somebody of his ethnicity as he progressed in his career. Now, there is no rule that says that this will always be the case. I have seen this happen more often than not, though.

There is another, not so altruistic reason, why this senior leader may give you some time, and that has to do with optics. Smart executives understand that turning your back on people like you is simply not a good look. What this means is that your networking should start with identifying powerful people with backgrounds similar to yours, because your barrier to entry is likely lower than that of others.

So, if you are Hispanic, for example, ALFA (Association of Latinos in Finance and Accounting) events are probably a more effective way to network than a generic finance event. To make the most of the opportunity, you should research who will be in attendance at the event. Identify who are the most senior and important executives who will be there, and send them a note beforehand to let them know you would like to introduce yourself while at the gathering.

Even if you don't get a response, the introduction at the event will be warm, because you have already reached out. Also, since out of sight is out of mind, it may take more than one introduction before you register on the person's mind. Building relationships that matter takes time. Lastly, your first networking introduction should never be to ask for a favor, a referral, or a job. Instead, you should use your precious networking time to ask questions and subtly impress upon your new contact that you are different, in a good way.

This type of selective "affinity" networking worked for me once, at a time when it was most needed. At the end of the 2000s, financial services was entering its worst crisis since the Great Depression. I was at the now defunct Wachovia (a very large financial institution based in Charlotte, North Carolina) where I led a team of more than seventy professionals charged with running the bank's massive website.

Earlier in the year, I had attended a Hispanic financial services networking event. In attendance was the head of diversity recruiting at rival Bank of America, also headquartered in Charlotte.

When I looked at the list of people who were to attend, I made it a point to meet Jose Garcia since I thought that, as the person charged with diverse talent acquisition for senior roles at the bank, he may be a great contact — if not at that moment, certainly in the future.

Things were going great at Wachovia. Then the financial crisis hit, and the company imploded spectacularly and was swiftly picked up by Wells Fargo. My entire team (in fact, the entire bank) was in a panic, as it was only obvious that massive layoffs were imminent. Big Wall Street firms were disappearing into thin air, the markets were in turmoil, and chaos was everywhere. Those who were there know that those were very scary times indeed.

On the morning that the media announced that Wells would be absorbing Wachovia, I came into the office to find several people from my team waiting for me at the office to ask me what was going to happen to their jobs. The fact was, I did not know, nor did I know what would happen to me. And then, amidst all the chaos and uncertainty, I got a call from my new friend, Jose Garcia, who wanted to let me know that a role had opened at Bank of America for an SVP of eMerchadising within the bank's digital marketing team.

The role involved managing the most important bank-owned digital marketing channels, would require no move, and came with a bump in compensation. Within a few days, I was interviewing and accepting a job offer for this new role. My selective networking had paid off.

The point here is simply that, if I had chosen to network randomly within the financial services circles of Charlotte, it is unlikely that an opportunity of this magnitude would have revealed itself. After all, at that time, there were literally hundreds of mid-level managers and director-level professionals looking for work in anticipation of the impending layoffs in the industry. But my contact at Bank of America, whose job was to find people just like me for senior roles, had a much smaller pool of candidates for his internal client's consideration set.

NOURISHING THE NETWORK TODAY, FOR TOMORROW

The reason we build extensive professional networks over time is so that, when the day comes when we need it—for example, to find our next opportunity—we can tap into all those connections. However, if you don't nourish your network when you don't need it, then when you do need to activate it, your networking may not be as effective.

IMPROBABLE FACT #3

If you don't reach out to your most valuable contacts when you don't need them, then when you do, your email or text will likely be received as just a favor from somebody in the past who never took the time to check in occasionally.

I fully recognize that reaching out at least once a year to the most influential people in your network is time-consuming and, in fact, may seem counterintuitive. After all, if you are happy in your current role with no plans to make changes in the near future, why would you take time to reach out to somebody just to "check in?" The answer is simply because a good business relationship is just like any other human relationship: You get out of it what you put into it.

Pretend that you belong to a large family, but you never reach out to them. When their kids graduate, somebody gets married, or a parent passes away, your family never hears from you. One day, you need a favor — one of those favors that perhaps only family can do for you — and, lo and behold, you reach out to your relatives to ask for help. How likely are they to assist when you neglected them for years?

Business is similar in that regard. An occasional, sincere "check-in" message with that VIP in your network, with no favors to ask, sends a message that you appreciate their business friendship. With these types of actions, you are building network "savings" that can be used in the future, when needed.

A similar strategy, but even more effective, is to go out of your way to help a fellow professional when they reach out to you asking for help. I always welcome a call, text, or LinkedIn message from somebody in my network reaching out for help because they have lost their job or want to know if I can connect them with somebody who can help them land their dream job. I like receiving these types of inquiries, because I sincerely love helping people in these situations. Very few things give me so much joy as assisting, in any way I can, somebody who is looking to make a professional move.

Work is very important for most of us so enabling employment, for me, is a meaningful way to have a positive impact in somebody's life. As it turns out, though, helping somebody can also yield rewards for yourself down the road. Most people will always remember those who genuinely helped at a stressful time and, in most cases, are willing to return the favor. So, when somebody reaches out to you seeking help, do not look at the request as a nuisance and ignore it. Look at it as an opportunity to help a colleague and gain an advocate. The day may come when your contact can provide the special introduction, connection, or insight that you need to land your next gig.

FORESHADOWING OPPORTUNITY

As we covered earlier, most things worth building require careful planning. Your career is no different. So a great career strategy is what I call "foreshadowing networking." This approach starts with visualizing a role or a company where you really want to work, followed by a well thought-out plan to meet somebody who is in a position to help you get that role in the future.

A good friend of mine who worked at a mid-sized bank had always dreamed of working at Goldman Sachs. When she was in college, she heard about the great pay and prestige at the firm, but as much as she tried to get an internship or an entry-level job at Goldman

Sachs, she simply did not have what they were looking for at that time. This was a source of frustration for her, because she knew she had the talent and brains to work there, but she did not have the Ivy League education, experience, or connections to get in.

Over time, though, she landed roles with increasing levels of responsibility and, as she approached mid-career, she decided that this time she would get in. The challenge was that, by then, she had "fallen behind" others with more experience in corporate and investment banking at competing firms who, therefore, had an edge over her. At this point, she realized that her best shot would be to get to know somebody on the inside who could champion her candidacy when the right opportunity would come along.

But she also understood that meaningful business relationships take time to build. So her strategy involved researching who, within Goldman Sachs, met two criteria. One, the contact had to have something in common with her so that it would be natural to connect and network and, two, the person had to be in a position to possibly help one day by circulating her résumé to a hiring manager or facilitating an introduction.

So my friend got busy and discovered a person at the firm who had attended the same college as she, was also a female and worked in the executive talent acquisition team at Goldman Sachs. The first step was sending a simple LinkedIn connection request to a prospective contact who quickly accepted. She followed up with a message introducing herself and pointing out how they had some commonalities. She also suggested that, one day, they connect over the phone. No favors, just casual professional networking.

Over the ensuing months, my friend would send the occasional "check in" LinkedIn message and promise that, if she were ever in New

York, she would let her new contact know so that, perhaps, they'd get together for coffee or lunch. Rather than superficial "small talk" exchanges, the occasional check-ins would be used to share industry information or provide updates on career updates, such as an interesting new project. The idea was to share information that was meaningful, understanding that people are very busy and normally do not use LinkedIn as a social "chat" channel.

The following year, my friend had to go to New York for a conference and, with three months advance notice, she asked her Goldman Sachs connection for a lunch date, which materialized. Again, she didn't ask any favors during lunch. She did share that she had always been intrigued at the idea of working at Goldman Sachs, but nothing more. During lunch, they hit it off because, as it is often the case, they had more in common than not.

By then, my friend had developed a solid, honest business networking relationship with a colleague who could one day help. And that's exactly what happened. A few months after the New York lunch, my friend became aware of an opportunity at Goldman Sachs for a role that would represent a step up in her career, with a pathway for a significant improvement in compensation and level. Naturally, my friend reached out to her contact at the firm and, without even asking, her new contact offered to help. Within a week, my friend was on the phone with the hiring manager and, three weeks after that, she received a job offer.

Now, mind you, this process from beginning to end took almost two years, and it required time and effort, but it 100% worked. Now, somebody may argue that this was a very calculated move. My counter argument would be that this was simply solid career planning with an outcome in which the candidate, her recruiting friend, and the hiring firm all benefited. So as you think about your next move or dream job, start thinking (and acting) on how you can be strategic and deliberate with your professional networking.

CHAPTER 5

YOUR PROFESSIONAL BRAND

Famed political consultant and strategist Lee Atwater once proclaimed that "perception is reality." In my experience, when it comes to your personal professional brand, that is indeed true. Good or bad, so much of our careers depends on how we are perceived and how we manage our image. This is why it is important to care for the most important brand you will ever manage: yours.

One thing that has struck me in all the years that I've been in the corporate world is how little awareness there is of this fact, even amongst the most brilliant professionals. That's unfortunate, because I have seen how average performers can advance their careers exponentially by carefully grooming their professional brands.

In this chapter, we will focus on how to best manage your presence on LinkedIn and other social media, and we will touch on the importance of growing your brand through speaking engagements. Finally, we will explore effective strategies to improve your executive presence and discuss why corporate titles are so important to your success.

YOUR LINKEDIN PROFILE

A few years back, I was talking to the COO of a mid-sized, regional bank about LinkedIn. He said to me, "I'm not in the job market, and LinkedIn is for people who are looking for work." A few years later, I had a similar conversation with a bank CEO. He shared with me that he never went on LinkedIn, because all he got out of it were incessant sales pitches.

Neither of these two very senior leaders were 100% wrong. As of the writing of this book, LinkedIn continues to be a great tool for finding your next job. However, it is also true that, if you have a "C" in front of your title or are perceived as managing a meaningful budget for your area of expertise, you will get dozens of invitations to connect from sales professionals. But until somebody comes up with a better tool, LinkedIn remains the most effective way to establish and build your professional brand.

LinkedIn is very powerful, because it features the ability to network, publish, and keep current your résumé; seek opportunities; and establish thought leadership, all in one place. And, since it is primarily a business social network, it makes it easy to avoid the potential pitfalls that come with networks like Facebook and Instagram. You control the message, your visual image, and how you are perceived. And, best of all, you can do all this for free, even if you do not sign up for a Premium membership.

So what are the best practices and strategies to get the most out of LinkedIn? Let's start with your profile. Your LinkedIn profile has a number of standard sections that include your job history and a profile picture. There is also a background image and several optional fields that can help tell your story.

Starting with your profile photo, I am always surprised to see very smart, successful professionals who use personal and not-so-flattering pictures of themselves on LinkedIn. I've seen profile pictures that include a pet, some with Hawaiian shirts, and some that are blurry beyond recognition. The problem with these images is that even the most impressive résumé cannot erase the first impression that your profile photo delivers. Such images tell the world that either you don't care or you don't get it. Neither of these is the right message to convey if you are trying to project yourself as a pro. Another common mistake I often see is that people post a picture from two decades ago or more. While I understand that many of us prefer a younger version of ourselves, when people (say a prospective employer), meets this year's version of you, they may also start wondering about what else you may be hiding. Worse yet, they may wonder why you don't like the way you look today.

If you are not crazy about your current professional photo, many employers offer a "photo day" for employees who are in mid-management and above levels. If you work for a company that provides this, be sure to take advantage of it. If this is not a possibility, there are a number of very affordable apps that can take your standard selfie and convert it into a professional photo for LinkedIn and other uses. One such application is Secta Labs, which takes regular pictures, even those with other people in them, and converts them into professional pictures.

And for those who have two or more pictures and you don't know which one to use, websites like Photofeeler.com allow you to upload your pictures so that other members of the site can provide you objective feedback based on set criteria. Lastly, whatever you do, please do not keep a LinkedIn profile with no picture at all.

In addition to a professional, current profile picture, the "About" section of your profile is important as it provides a summary of who you are as a professional. There are dozens of blog articles on how to write an effective "About" LinkedIn section, so we will touch on just three essentials:

1. Make it **concise**. Recruiters and hiring managers are not particularly interested in reading your biography. They want

to get the key facts about your skills and professional trajectory to determine if you are a good fit for the role they seek to fill.

2. Keep it **factual**. Ensure that everything you write in this section is actually matched with who you are and what you can bring to your ideal future role. If you claim to be an effective communicator, please be sure you are indeed both effective and a communicator. If you say you are a strategic thinker, please ensure that comes through at the time of the interview and you do not get mired in tactical details.

3. Leverage **keywords**. Please remember that LinkedIn is, in addition to everything else above, a powerful search engine. Be thoughtful and deliberate about the adjectives and words you use in your profile so that you can be found by those looking for candidates with those attributes.

As for the "Experience" section, it is always a good idea to cite tangible, measurable results for each role you've held, rather than using general descriptions about the job. If you are a risk analyst, there's no need to describe in minute detail what your job entails. Instead, talk about the business impact of the role or, even better, use a quantifier that helps the reader understand the scope of both your role and the organization.

This last point is particularly important if you work for a company that does not have a recognizable, famous brand. For example, some years back I worked as CMO for the U.S. arm of Rabobank, a large Dutch bank. Unless you are in banking, and especially in agricultural finance, and you are in the U.S., chances are you've never heard of Rabobank. So I made sure to add that this was a global financial institution with 600 billion dollars in assets. That way, whoever reads that part of my experience knows that Rabobank is a major, international company.

As for how many years of work history to add to "Experience," my recommendation is to include only that which is necessary. Having thirty-plus years in this section can actually hurt you in sectors like technology where, let's be honest, ageism sometimes occurs. A simple rule to follow is to understand what, on average, is the number of years of experience needed for the type of role you are seeking, and don't go back in time much further than that. For example, if you are mid-career and employers typically look for ten to fifteen years of experience for your desired role, don't go back to your just-out-of-college internship.

The exception to this rule, of course, is if you are just starting your career. If you are under thirty, it makes sense to put all your experience — even that summer retail job — in there. Employers understand that you are just starting your career, and there's no shame in adding entry-level jobs that you had when you were just getting going.

Regarding the "Education" section of LinkedIn, if you have a college degree, there is no need to keep your high school education in this section, even if you went to high school at a top, prestigious private school.

What does help is to add any certificates and non-degree training that is relevant to your profession. This strategy is particularly effective if you pursue and complete continuing education from highly prestigious institutions that can help enhance your educational profile.

In my case, for example, I earned my undergraduate business degree from California State University in Los Angeles (not to be confused with the much better-known University of California, Los Angeles or UCLA). Cal State L.A. is a great state school that attracts mostly working class, minority students that typically commute to school. For me, it was a great option, as I had neither the grades nor the financial means to attend a more prestigious school. I then attended Pepperdine University to pursue my MBA, a school with a better known "brand" than Cal State L.A. But later in my career came the opportunity to go to Oxford for a continuing education program in global enterprise management. So now I've got Oxford in my profile, along with another continuing ed certificate in Innovation Management from Stanford. All of these educational experiences come together in my LinkedIn profile showing schools across the prestige spectrum, but all in the areas of business, marketing and innovation, which is what I have always loved and do for a living.

LinkedIn features sections for things like patents, honors, awards, and recommendations which can really round out your profile, especially if you have gaps in other parts of your profile.

IMPROBABLE FACT #4

According to the U.S. Census Bureau, only about 20% of all Americans speak more than one language. If you happen to be one of them, please be sure to make that known in your LinkedIn profile. In an increasingly globalized economy, the more languages you speak, the better. This is true at every stage of your career. More on this topic later on in this book.

Lastly, you should take full advantage of LinkedIn's publishing capabilities, using posts. If you follow some simple rules, you can easily build a following on the network and get more of them to see your posts. Terry Heath, COO and LinkedIn strategist from Maverrik, a leading digital and social selling agency, studied the performance of LinkedIn posts and came up with the following tips to grow post engagement and audience:

- Post posts, not long articles
- Use PDF slides (fewer than ten slides)
- Use video
- Focus on entertaining and educational posts
- Publish LinkedIn polls
- Post regularly
- Do not overindulge with tags
- Reply to comments on your posts

By using these best practices and being thoughtful about the topics you post about, you can build your thought leadership and your professional brand with those you want to influence.

Another proven strategy is to repost great content and add your two (smart) cents. This strategy also signals to potential employers that they can count on you to be a strong ambassador for their brand and business. Win-win!

OTHER SOCIAL MEDIA

When social media started taking off, it brought with it the opportunity to reconnect and stay in touch with friends and relatives. It also allowed us to meet people who shared our interests and to participate in forums where we could partake in open discussions about almost any topic.

However, social media also means that most of your comments, likes, rants, and connections are captured somewhere in the cloud for posterity. This, of course, is potentially problematic for professionals who want to manage their brands. You hear it every day: careers down the drain because somebody found an old, controversial tweet or photo lying somewhere deep in the archives of your favorite social platform.

Recognizing that it is difficult to separate our personal and professional online selves, here are some tips on how to make popular, non-business networks work for you as you advance your career, followed by some things you can do to protect your brand online.

Twitter / X

Many feel that X is for celebrities, professional athletes, politicians, and other public figures. Why put all that work into tweeting when most of our tweets can get one or two likes, on a good day? The reason is simply because Twitter is a space where you can establish thought leadership and build your professional reputation with a minimal time investment. Just like LinkedIn, Tweeter/X can get your name out there, the way you want it, in the public domain, while making you look smart and plugged into your business.

Best of all, you don't need tens of thousands of followers and massive engagement. In terms of career management, you are really tweeting for the day when that recruiter or hiring manager Googles your name and they see that, not only you are an authority in your field, but that you are also smart enough to understand the concept of managing your professional brand. Just as with LinkedIn, you may also earn some points with your current employer if you retweet their content, thus becoming a true brand ambassador for them. If you are going to share your employer's posts, be sure to check that the company's policies allow you to do so without prior approval. Since some of us share and post personal and work-related content, it is also a good idea to add to your profile a disclaimer stating that your opinions are not necessarily those of your employer.

To help you with managing this part of your professional brand, here are what I call the X5 strategies:

THE X5: MANAGING FOR X / TWITTER PROFESSIONAL BRAND	
No inspiration? No problem	Retweet great content from brands, organizations, and individuals with great reputations and simply add a short commentary or hashtag. Many people will think you are smart if you occasionally retweet content from handles like Harvard Business Review (@HarvardBiz) or MIT Technology Review (@techreview).
Watch who you follow	Depending on your account's settings, on Twitter, the public can see the list of those handles you follow. You may want to stay away from following controversial accounts that can hint at, for example, your political leanings. I have known cases of job offers being pulled at the last minute because the hiring manager discovers the otherwise dream candidate has radical views that are likely to create toxicity in the workplace. We are all entitled to our opinions and have the freedom to speak out loud about them, but be sure to choose wisely where you do that. In addition, in those social media channels that allow you to do so, you can simply adjust your settings so that the people you follow won't be visible to the public.
Be constant	Tweet on a regular cadence, and don't abandon your handle; you would be surprised what some people can read into abandonment... Oh, and tweeting with some frequency helps build your follower base over time.
Play tag!	Be sure to tag organizations, brands, and individuals with large follower bases. This also applies to things like trending hashtags and events you are attending. This tactic will help you build your audience over time and will deliver the message that you understand how Twitter works.
Avoid controversy	While it is always tempting to engage in Twitter political wars, such behavior can send the wrong message about the kind of person you are.

Instagram, Facebook, and others

Many of us maintain a presence in social media channels like Instagram and Facebook for a variety of reasons. From a career management point of view, the guidance on using these "social" social media is relatively simple.

Always assume that everything that you post is 100% public, even if your profiles are locked down and, in theory, only accessible to those you allow in. Why? Because anybody in your network can take a screenshot of what you post and post that. Once you make this assumption, then always ask yourself, before you post anything, if that content could potentially come back to haunt you.

Once I was talking to a friend who is in the recruiting business, and she shared with me that a standard part of their candidate vetting process is to Google the person and look at their social media presence. She went on to tell me that they specifically look for content posted by the candidate that may indicate that the person may be controversial or toxic once on the job.

The message here is clear: If you are in social media, watch what you post and be aware of who can and cannot see this content. If it is very important for you to be active in online forums for topics that you feel passionate about (say, politics), you can always set up a separate account that cannot be readily associated with you. A second account with a different name and profile picture allows you to be vocal about potentially controversial topics, while protecting your professional image.

Additionally, if you are in the job market and you have a fairly public social media presence, it may be wise to go back through your timeline and ensure that there are no posts from the past that may be objectionable or controversial to a prospective employer or recruiter. If you do find posts that may be offensive to potential employers, consider deleting them.

Lastly, if you work in an area that requires creativity (for example, design), you should indeed use a channel like Instagram to post some of your best work. Same goes for realtors, architects, and other professions where visuals are important.

SPEAKING ENGAGEMENTS

Sometime back, when I worked at a Miami digital marketing agency, I was charged with driving sales through activities like cold calling and asking existing clients for referrals. These tactics were effective, but they came with long sales cycles and a low ratio of sales calls to closed deals. We then realized that south Florida was quickly becoming the epicenter of Latin American e-commerce and internet conferences. These large gatherings, held at hotels near the beach or the airport, attracted marketing and technology professionals from Latin America who worked for large companies and wanted to stay current on how to use the web to grow their businesses.

It occurred to us, in the agency, that these conferences could be great "hunting grounds" for us because, in many cases, conference delegates worked with companies large enough and with deep enough pockets to send their executives to the U.S. to learn about the latest and greatest digital trends. These folks had budgets! But how could we get in front of them so that they would know we existed and could help? The answer was simple: find a way to speak at the conferences.

The problem was that, in most cases, event organizers wanted a fee from vendors to get on the agenda, or they wanted speakers from established, marquee brands. Our answer: develop such great presentations, often focused on real-life case studies from our clients, that it would be hard to turn us away. Oh, and we had another secret weapon: We could deliver the presentation in Spanish as part of an in-language track, which invariably worked because all things being equal, folks prefer to take in information in their native language. Using your native language, if it is anything other than English, can be a great differentiator, as we cover in another chapter of this book. This strategy worked, and our agency quickly became a fixture of the Miami/Latin America digital speaking circle, which resulted in prospects actually approaching us after a presentation to learn about our services.

Speaking works for business, and it can work for you as part of a strategy to grow and sustain your professional brand for several reasons. First, it can help establish you as a subject matter expert within your industry in a very efficient manner. This gets your name out in the marketplace and builds your network. Second, it can help you build confidence to speak, with authority, in front of any audience. If you can speak in front of 300 people, you can certainly speak in the boardroom. Third, when combined with your personal social media, it can be a powerful professional brand building strategy.

The truth is, however, that not everyone is comfortable with speaking in front of groups, especially a large one made up of your peers and prospective employers. Over the years, I have met brilliant professionals who are true experts in their fields but are simply terrified of public speaking. It's also a fact that an extrovert who is perfectly comfortable with speaking in front of thousands can fall flat if the topic is irrelevant or the content of the talk is just not that relevant.

So let's explore strategies to help you address these potential stumbling blocks.

First, we will start with the challenge of fear and discomfort with public speaking. I have had professional motivational speakers confess to me that even they get nervous before a speaking engagement. My own brother, who was a professional musician for decades, concurred. He has shared with me that even the most seasoned performer gets jittery before hitting the stage.

However, the one thing that can really help that feeling of nervousness before and during a public talk is being fully prepared. Even if you know the subject like the palm of your hand, you should always have notes and rehearse (even if the rehearsal is just in your mind) as part of your routine. This is particularly important if your presentation has facts and figures in it, historical references or names of people. Preparation gives you confidence which in turn makes you comfortable in front of an audience.

Another tactic that can help you get comfortable as you deliver your presentation is opening with a personal anecdote, especially if it is funny. This approach helps "break the ice" and can create a personal connection quickly so that you can get into the essence of your content. One word of caution, though: If you are going to use humor, any time during your speaking engagement, ensure that it is not potentially offensive to members of your audience.

A few years back, at the annual sales and marketing hosted by a financial institution I worked for, a motivational speaker hired for the event opened with a politically charged joke. My supposition is that he was trying to read the audience and guessed that particular joke would appeal to his audience. Unfortunately, his gamble did not pay off. Even though many found his opening joke to be hilarious, at least 30% of the audience did not and, in fact, took offense to it. This meant that, two minutes into his forty-five-minute presentation, our speaker was already in a situation where we had to convince a good part of his audience that he was not a jerk....

Lastly, one thing that can help you stay calm and focused during a presentation is to find that one person in the audience who is fully engaged, and maybe even nodding, and establish visual contact with that person. To you, it feels like a one-on-one conversation. Naturally, great public speakers engage the entire room and scan left to right and back, establishing eye contact with as many people in the audience as possible. But, to help you get comfortable, you can start with the one audience member who you know or feel an instant connection with, and build from there.

AMPLIFYING YOUR SPEAKING ENGAGEMENT

Another great professional benefit of a solid speaking engagement strategy is that these presentation opportunities can be amplified beyond the actual event to support your overall personal brand. For example, using your professional social media accounts to let the world know about your speaking engagement can be a powerful way to build your reputation as a subject matter expert. Ideally, your post will have your picture on stage. You should tag your host's social media handle and those of your co-presenters, if you are part of a panel.

In addition, if the conference organizers created a hashtag for the event, be sure to add it to your post for greater exposure and to subliminally let the world know that you understand how professional social media works.

Lastly, if you want your audience to connect with you after your speaking engagement, you can add a call-to-action at the end of your presentation, encouraging event attendees to connect with / follow you on LinkedIn and X/Twitter. If you want these connections to take place in real time, you can add a QR code, like this one, that points to your LinkedIn profile on your closing slide.

There are multiple websites that allow you to create a personalized QR quote for free and in seconds. This one was created using qrcode-monkey.com.

YOUR EXECUTIVE PRESENCE

I have always been intrigued by the notion of executive presence. In a *Forbes* article, executive coach Gerry Valentine described executive presence as "the ability to inspire confidence," and I tend to agree with this simple definition. In your career, you have probably met professionals who simply project confidence through their behavior, communication style, and appearance.

The first question to ask on this topic is whether we think that having a strong executive presence can make a difference in our careers. Or would it simply be a nice thing for our ego, but with no tangible positive impact on our career? My strong opinion, which is founded on three decades of observing those with successful careers, is that executive presence does, in fact, impact one's success.

However, before we discuss the specifics of developing and projecting a strong executive presence, we have to deconstruct the concept and be clear on what it is not. For some, an executive presence is synonymous with certain traditional stereotypes of what a top executive looks like. If, when you hear "top executive" or CEO, you imagine a clean cut, slim, tall male of northern European descent is what comes to mind, then it is time to reassess your perception of executive presence. Same with females: If you are thinking slender, White, and a Chanel power suit, then you would be wise to question that notion as well.

Where did these stereotypes come from? The answer is simple. They come from, one, the undeniable fact that historically and statistically, in the West, top executives have indeed looked like that and, two, the fact that Western media has reinforced this image over decades. But the fact is that, today, that stereotype no longer holds, even in places like North America and Europe. The world has changed, and top executives are a reflection of the increasingly global world of business. So if you have ever doubted that you could have the gravitas to lead in the workplace because you don't look like a CEO from a 1960s TV show, it is time to move on and understand that executive presence is not about height, ethnic background, or the pedigree of the university you attended. It is all about your behavior, your emotional intelligence, and your ability to apply your brain power and abilities to influence, inspire, and motivate others to act.

That is not to say that your appearance is not important, because it is. But it is important to understand that appearance is but one dimension of executive presence and that such appearance does not have to be defined by historical or media-driven stereotypes.

On this point, I want to share my own personal experience. At 5 feet and 7 inches, with darker skin and a mixed-race background, I do not look like what comes up when you search stock images using the keywords "American executive." And yet, over the past twenty-plus years, I have more than held my own with fellow executives and in boardrooms. Why? Simply because I have never associated my ability to lead and succeed with my physical self. To me, it has always been about the self confidence that comes with knowing your trade and having the conviction to know that you can effectively lead yourself and others.

And it's not just me. Over the years, I have had the opportunity to work with and for exceptional leaders, of all genders, who are as diverse as the world we live in, but who all have certain common traits. What are those things, then, that make up executive presence? Here is my list of traits, in no particular order:

Gravitas—Gravitas is when you are taken seriously and, as a result, you can more easily persuade others and influence outcomes. Professionals with gravitas are not the ones who talk all the time or the ones who try too hard to be the smartest person in the room. You can enhance your gravitas with command of the facts, developing your own point of view based on those facts and, ultimately, communicating all that in an assertive and direct manner.

Communication—Great leaders and executives are often effective communicators. They communicate clearly, concisely, and with confidence. They are also consistent while adapting their message according to the audience, be it the board of directors or the summer interns during their orientation. Great communication is a learned skill that anybody can master. Best of all, great communication is not a one-size-fits-all skill. In fact, great communicators leverage their personality and personal background to deliver messages that are authentic. So, while very few of us are likely to achieve the oratory abilities of someone like

Barack Obama, each of us can certainly use what makes us unique and combine it with best practices to communicate in a personal and effective manner. More on this important topic later on in this book.

Appearance—Here again, it is important to note that there is not one "uniform" that we can simply buy at the store to achieve instant executive presence. Having said that, it is also true that people make instant, subconscious judgments about our professional person based on things like attire and grooming. After attending literally hundreds of business meetings over my thirty-year career, I have consistently noticed how people in a room conduct a millisecond scan of people as they walk in. In that instant, they register things like the shoes you wear, whether you are wearing certain brands, if your clothes fit you properly, your hair (or lack of), and even things like whether you are wearing a wedding ring or not.

All these things get processed, subconsciously, in seconds and you are instantly given a label, based on set stereotypes and cultural norms. In peoples' heads, they say things like "she looks so smart," "he looks like he doesn't care," "look at that slit skirt; this one is trouble," or "his nails are painted black . . . oh, I get it!" We can argue whether these instant judgment calls are fair or not, but the fact remains that they are a reality in work settings.

Without getting into specifics, the general advice here is simply to be mindful of who else will be at the meeting or in the video call, and ensure that your appearance matches how you want to be perceived. As Austin Kleon, a bestselling author on creativity, famously said, "You have to dress for the job you want, not the job you have." Naturally, and yet once again, this does not mean that we all have to wear pinstripe suits and Chanel dresses. Our appearance can be an extension of our authentic selves. Some years back, I worked for an African American executive who had an amazing collection of African scarfs and head wraps, which she combined with traditional dresses, resulting in an incredibly professional appearance that also proudly accentuated her heritage. The way she dressed projected confidence and professionalism in a very personal and genuine way.

Posture / Body Language — Similarly to appearance, our posture and body language say a lot about who we are as professionals and our ability to project a strong executive presence. Once again, we humans appear to be programmed to read other's body language and inform our opinions about them in nanoseconds. Pretend that you are making a presentation to executive management and, as you walk into the room, you are slightly slouched, walking slowly with near zero eye contact. What kind of signal do you suppose that would send to those in front of you? That's right: You are unsure of yourself, or maybe you do not even want to be there. At that point, you are already at a disadvantage even if the contents of your presentation are very compelling.

Professionals with a strong executive presence project optimism and confidence using their bodies, their gestures, and their demeanor. Some things I have observed peers do consistently to assert their presence include:

- Walk upright and at a steady pace. Too slow, and you are telling them you do not have a sense of urgency. Too fast, and you are telling them you are hyperactive or nervous.

- Do not over-gesture. One time, my boss, the CEO of the company, actually asked me to stop waving my hands so much to underscore points I was trying to make.

Unbeknownst to me, all of my hand gestures were distracting the person in front of me, which undermined what I was attempting to communicate. Apparently, the time I worked at an agency, where the vast majority of my colleagues were from Argentina (and of southern European descent) had rubbed off on me, and nobody told me that I was overdoing it until that very embarrassing moment.

- Much has been written about the signal that crossing your arms sends. It seems the consensus is that arms crossing indicates to the other party that you are not open to whatever is being communicated. Essentially, it is a non-verbal wall, so be aware of when you are about to cross your arms — and stop yourself.

- Touching your hair, nose, and other parts of your face frequently denotes nervousness and insecurity. Sometimes, we do this without being aware. One of the good things that have come out of the now-common video call is that we can see ourselves on-screen, and it can help us catch these behaviors which is the first step in making any necessary corrections.

- Direct and focused eye contact is always best, because it tells others that you are genuinely interested in what they have to say. The opposite, which is to avoid looking others into their eyes, can sometimes make others feel a sense of distrust and wonder what you are hiding.

Assertiveness — Assertiveness is the quality in professionals that allows them to project the feeling that they are sure of their actions and their words. Effective executives rarely hesitate, even when they don't have all the answers, because they have the ability to project immense credibility.

One time, I was attending a meeting where senior executives and mid-managers were discussing the business value of a certain feature in the bank's mobile banking solution. A question came up about adoption of the app within a certain segment, and one of the managers in the room actually had the answer at his fingertips. However, when he spoke, there was a bit of hesitation on his voice, which got worse when a follow-up question was asked. It was clear, at that moment, that the meeting participants were doubtful of the manager's domain of the subject, and as extension of that, his competence.

After this brief exchange, the executive sponsor of the initiative interjected and, looking assertively around the room, took over the conversation and very quickly gave direction on how and by when to validate the data, what next steps would be based on what the analysis would reveal, and who would be in charge of what. As you looked around the room, you could see several people nodding in approval. Incidentally, I have seen colleagues use this approach, regardless of their level within the organization. Assertiveness is not the exclusive domain of executives. It is a learned behavior that anybody can master.

Like some personal traits, executive presence is sometimes difficult to self-ascertain, and there may well be differences between how we perceive ourselves and how others see us. We may think that we project a strong executive presence, while our peers may see us as "work in progress," or worse. The best way to identify potential blind spots in this area is to ask for feedback formally or informally. A popular tool for getting this type of input is through 360-degree feedback surveys, which is offered by many large employers. Just as useful and insightful is the feedback that a mentor, a peer, or a supervisor can provide. This more informal source of feedback can be immensely helpful when offered candidly and with the right intention. Either way, if you have the opportunity to get feedback on just how strong your executive presence is, do so.

Here are these five executive presence traits captured in a simple diagram:

THE FIVE EXECUTIVE PRESENCE TRAITS

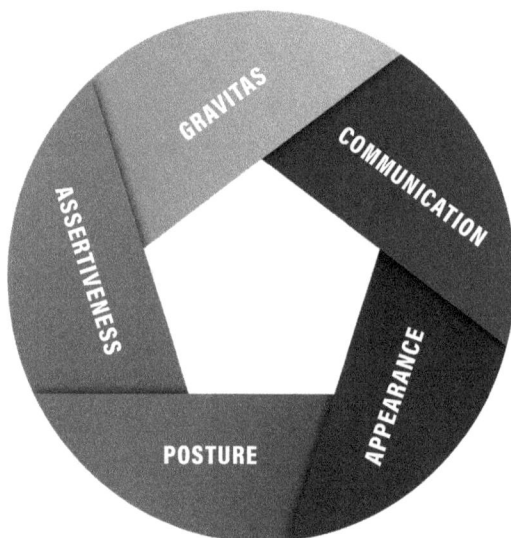

CORPORATE TITLES AND WHY THEY MATTER

In this section of the book, we will discuss the importance of corporate titles as it pertains to upward mobility. The idea is simply this: It is in your best interest to work towards the most senior title you can earn, because that becomes the baseline for your next job.

This may seem obvious, but I am always surprised by co-workers who tell me things like, "I don't care about my title as long as I get to do what I love." As much as I admire this kind of altruism, the fact remains that, in most industries, bigger titles come with bigger compensation.

Let's look at an industry that is notorious for corporate title inflation: financial services. In financial institutions like banks, for example, an assistant vice president can be a relatively junior professional with five years or less experience. Then comes vice president which, in many banks, is a lower-level supervisory role. So a vice president of marketing at a financial institution could be someone supervising fewer than ten people, or could even be an individual contributor. By contrast, in tech, a vice president of marketing could well be the head of marketing for the entire enterprise, and the equivalent of a chief marketing officer. The gap in pay between these two vice presidents could be as much as hundreds of thousands of dollars per year. But a bank employee with a vice president title on her résumé can aspire to a much bigger role if she switches industries, because she now has the vice president title under her belt.

Just as important for this professional is that now that she has earned that VP title, she is not likely to take a new role with a lesser title. Her trajectory is now set, and her goal is to become a senior vice president. The implication here from a career management point of view is that, as professionals, we should negotiate corporate titles as hard as we negotiate compensation or any other aspects of a new job offer or promotion.

IMPROBABLE FACT #5

Corporate title is key as we manage our careers, because it is an indicator of growing responsibility, which is something that many recruiters and hiring managers like to see when they are evaluating job candidates. Few things look better on your résumé or LinkedIn profile than showing bigger job titles over the course of time. This kind of progression tells the world that you grow professionally as you go from assignment to assignment, and that you are a high potential individual. So, everything else aside, look for and take on opportunities with the bigger corporate title, even if it means giving up something else in the short term.

CHAPTER 6

COMMUNICATION: THE MASTER SKILL

I t has been my experience over three decades in leadership roles that no other skill can have a greater positive impact on your career than being able to communicate effectively.

If you observe work settings closely, you will notice that those leaders who can communicate better, verbally and in writing, often progress to roles of greater responsibility relative to their peers who have the same (or greater) subject matter expertise. Warren Buffett, one of the greatest investors and business people of the last century, once asserted, "The one easy way to become worth 50% more than you are now—at least—is to hone your communications skills—both written and verbal."

In this chapter, we are going to explore several practical strategies to help you improve your communication skills which, in turn, will help you grow professionally.

INSTANT CREDIBILITY WITH FACTS AND FIGURES

Even if you are still working on mastering communication overall, you can improve your abilities in this area by simply mastering facts and figures in your industry and your immediate area of responsibility. Speaking—and writing—with relevant facts means you are contributing information that can move conversations forward and inform decision-making.

Knowing your stuff and the source of your information makes you that much more effective, even if you are still working on things like assertiveness and acquiring an extensive lexicon. As a bonus, mastery of the facts (especially those that are numerical in nature) gives you instant credibility.

When I worked at a digital marketing start-up in south Florida, back in the nascent days of the commercial internet, large companies were trying to make sense of this new wondrous technology and how they should respond to it. Instinctively, they all knew this was going to be transformative, but they were not sure exactly how to capitalize on it. Was this a new powerful branding tool? Could it be leveraged to improve customer service? What about e-commerce? Perhaps all of the above.

My job at the new company was to prospect new customers and sell them our services (back in the day, it was mostly about building their very first website). We were fortunate to be a Microsoft Certified Partner, which gave us access to some smart engineers at their main campus in Redmond, Washington and, locally, in Miami at their Latin American headquarters. That meant we received product previews and got our hands on things like Microsoft's Commerce Server, their first technology designed to help enterprises build online stores.

Back then, I was a marketing person. Being exposed to technical folks who were at the forefront of the web allowed me to learn and, in turn, explain to prospective customers the basics of this new thing called the "web." Further, I could partner with them in conceiving a strategy that made sense, and that, of course, we could help them build. Knowing the technical facts, as very few did in the early days of the internet, allowed us to sign up as customers some of the biggest brands with headquarters in south Florida and to eventually expand our business to more than 150 consultants with offices in New York and Atlanta.

WRITING WELL

At the time of writing this book, generative AI and tools like Chat-GPT are the hot technology *du jour*. Even if, by the time you read these words, the buzz around this next generation of artificial intelligence has passed, the fact remains that tools that can emulate human writing are here to stay and will only get increasingly sophisticated. Still, if you want to progress in your career, you need to be able to write well. There's just no way around it.

Jeff Bradford, a former journalist with thirty-plus years of experience as a public relations professional and Forbes Councils member, argues in one of his articles that all forms of communications, from writing emails to speaking and blogging, require good writing skills. According to Mr. Bradford, this is so because "good writing is fundamentally good thinking that follows a logical path and is easy for someone to follow. Writing out what you want to communicate forces you to organize your thoughts."

My personal experience in this area fully supports his assertion. Further, I have observed that many highly effective professionals and business leaders are strong writers and often prefer to write their own communications, even if they have the services of an entire communications department at their disposal. One of the reasons this is often the case is because a "ghost writer," even an excellent one, can seldom capture the true voice of somebody else. After all, our communication style is a result of our background, education, and personality.

But what does it take to be an effective writer in a business setting? Here are four things that have worked for me:

1. **Be concise.** When it comes to writing, sometimes less is more. People's attention spans keep getting shorter, and they want to get to your point quickly.

2. **Be deliberate.** Before you start writing, be it an email or a white paper, ask yourself: What exactly is the point my written communication needs to deliver? If you are not 100% sure, think for a few minutes before you write the first word.

3. **Be precise.** Like most modern languages, English offers a very large number of words that can define, with a high degree of precision, the exact idea you are trying to get across. As you expand your vocabulary, precision becomes easier.

4. **Be professional.** Sometimes, we think that, because we are texting a colleague, we can be as informal as when we are texting friends and family. This is simply not the case. Whether you are writing an old-school memo, an instant message, or an email, always use the magic words: please and thank you (more on this topic later on).

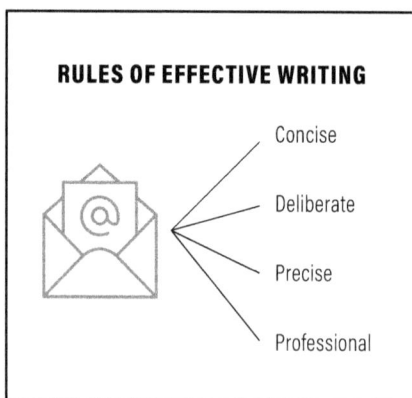

RULES OF EFFECTIVE WRITING

Concise

Deliberate

Precise

Professional

IMPROBABLE FACT #6

There is a clear correlation between good reading habits and strong writing skills. It seems that, the more we read, the better we write. This should come as no surprise, since reading feeds the brain by reminding you of words that are stored in your head but rarely used. Reading also teaches or reinforces your ability to effectively structure sentences and formulate ideas.

Listening to the right content via podcasts and audiobooks can help you become a better writer for reasons similar to those stated about reading. The operative word here, though, is "right," because just as there are books on every conceivable topic, there is audio content for every taste and topic. If your goal is to be a better business communicator, and your preference is to listen rather than read content, then be sure to subscribe to podcasts and get audiobooks featuring speakers who are subject matter experts in your area.

Growing Your Vocabulary.

Few things elevate your professional profile more than mastering your language and using it to be precise in your communications. This, in turn, advances your career potential. Professionals with extensive lexicons not only come across as more knowledgeable, but also as more intelligent (these are two different things). A growing vocabulary also makes you more efficient in both verbal and written communications, because using the right word allows you to convey the exact idea with fewer words.

As you develop and grow your vocabulary, there are three myths that you need to destroy.

Myth 1: You can only have an extensive vocabulary in your native language. The fact is that the human brain has an almost infinite capacity for adding new words (complete with their exact meaning) well into adulthood. One of the most eloquent masters of the English language I have ever listened to was my economics professor at Cal State L.A., who happened to be born and raised in South America. He seemed to always use the perfect word to explain complex ideas. And, yes, he had a South American accent, and English was very much his second language. Once, during office hours, I asked him (in Spanish, of course) how he managed to develop such mastery of the English language with such an extensive vocabulary. His answer surprised me. He explained to me that the English language was full of words that had roots in Latin and were widely used in say, Spanish, but very rarely used in English, and that happen to perfectly convey a specific thing or concept. These, he explained, were "free" words—words that he did not have to learn from scratch and that he started using once he established that the two versions of the word, Spanish and English, were the same. But how to actually establish the existence of these "free" words? Through reading, *naturalmente!*

Myth 2. Only attorneys and academia have extensive vocabularies. While it does seem that lawyers and college professors seem to have an endless source of jargon (words that are seldom used by anyone else), the fact is any of us can grow our own lexicon, even if we did not have access to law school or didn't earn a Ph.D. Some of the most articulate people I have met are public school teachers. Mrs.

Covington, my eighth-grade teacher, had this lyrical command of the English language filled with every expression that captured just the right concept. I was always mesmerized listening to her, hanging onto her every word. I am not sure where she went to college, but I would not be surprised if it were not Yale, and I do know she did not go to law school. She just loved English and the infinite possibilities that its tens of thousands of words provide to communicate effectively.

Myth 3. Using "fancy" words make you look conceited or snobbish. One time, I was having lunch with two workers, both people of color, when one of them threw a "big word" in the midst of the conversation. The other person, half-seriously and half-jokingly, jumped up and said, "Listen to you, sounding like some Ivy Leaguer or something…." The implication in the statement was that, somehow, owning an extensive vocabulary and being your authentic self cannot go hand in hand. This is a horrible myth that sadly still persists out there. The reality is that using the right word (even if it is a "big word") helps you be a better communicator and makes you look smart. So don't believe this myth.

So now that we have these fallacies out of the way, we can explore some additional real-life tactics and strategies that can help you grow your vocabulary.

- **Listen to smart, amazing communicators.** We are all fortunate to be alive at a time when, with the tap of a few buttons, we can access video and audio of some of the most eloquent people in the last decades. There are a lot of options out there, but for me, YouTube offers an amazing collection of lectures and debates from brilliant minds like Noam Chomsky, Willian F. Buckley, Jr., and Michael Sugrue. While you may or may not agree with their stances on various topics, listening to them speak is guaranteed to expand your vocabulary and train your brain to structure your thoughts and sentences.

- **Get hooked on Word of the Day.** Sites like Merriam-Webster.com offer a Word of the Day that allows you to subscribe for free to receive in your email a new word every day. This method or using one of a multitude of mobile apps that serve the same purpose, is a simple and fun way to learn (or relearn) great words that you can start using immediately.

- **Practice.** The point of acquiring new words is to use them in real-life conversations. So, if you pick up a new word, look for opportunities to use it that very same day and afterwards. You will then see that your new words become part of your day-to-day vocabulary.

LISTENING VS. TALKING: WHEN LESS IS MORE

As counterintuitive as it may sound, one of the most important communication skills actually involves doing less talking, which is the main thing that we associate with effective communications. It seems that much of the advice dispensed to improve our communication skills is related to things like clarity, tone, structure, etc. All of these practices support the act of talking. However, in order for two or more parties to exchange ideas and concepts, there must also be listening. But a lot of the literature related to communication tends to emphasize talking, not listening.

A simple search on YouTube will uncover hundreds of how-to videos on things like delivering presentations, being heard in meetings, and making convincing arguments. Unquestionably, all of these skills are important for professionals, but the secret to great communication does not actually involve talking. It's all about listening.

So why is great listening so important? Here are just some of the reasons:

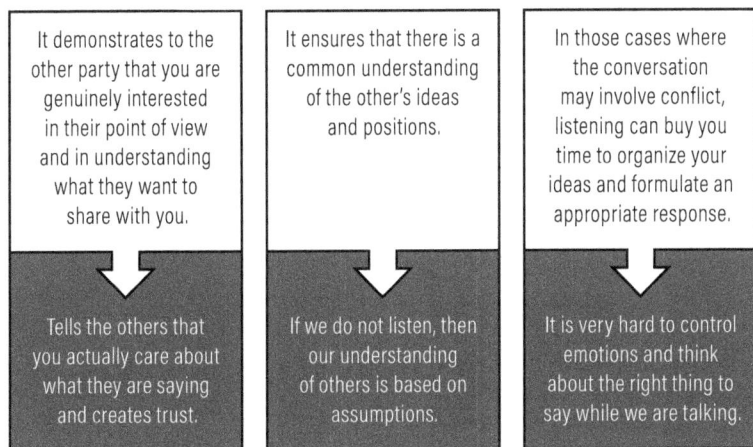

It demonstrates to the other party that you are genuinely interested in their point of view and in understanding what they want to share with you.	It ensures that there is a common understanding of the other's ideas and positions.	In those cases where the conversation may involve conflict, listening can buy you time to organize your ideas and formulate an appropriate response.
⬇	⬇	⬇
Tells the others that you actually care about what they are saying and creates trust.	If we do not listen, then our understanding of others is based on assumptions.	It is very hard to control emotions and think about the right thing to say while we are talking.

Some time back, I worked at a multinational firm with a large technology department, and one of my counterparts was the global head of IT architecture. He was a brilliant man, with a pedigreed education and decades of senior-level IT experience. His problem? A conversation with him was essentially a monologue. And, while much of what he said was actually interesting (if you like technology topics), the one-way nature of the conversation resulted in my tuning him out after a few minutes. Yes, I was there physically and even looking him in the eyes, but my mind was wandering. I was thinking about Sunday's game, a book I was reading, and what I was going to order for dessert.

In fact, and just for kicks, one night we went for a drink after work. I actually attempted to estimate the percentage of time he talked vs. the time I talked. Although I had no scientific way to measure the percentages (I would have had to use the stopwatch feature on my cell phone to do that), my best guess was that it was about 90% him and 10% me. And, in those few opportunities when I actually managed to get a word in, he interrupted me. While this was an extreme case, I am sure that you have met someone like that, and we can probably agree that those conversations, if we can call them that, were not fun. When we do all the talking and no listening, everything we have to say loses its value, and our credibility goes out the window.

ACTIVE LISTENING

There is one more important point about listening and that is that effective listening involves what is known as *active listening*. What exactly is active listening? It is listening while being fully present and engaged during a conversation. It also involves sending signals to the other party that you are capturing the message and understanding what is being communicated. Active listening requires reflecting which is restating, in your own words, the idea that you just heard to reassure the speaker that you fully understood what has been communicated to you.

Active listening also means asking follow-up questions to drive the communication forward and establishing direct, honest eye contact when the conversation involves two people.

It signals that you care, and that you are smart and empathetic. Successful professionals and leaders share the common behavior of active listening. If you are interested in perfecting your active listening skills, I recommend that you become familiar with the six steps for more effective active listening from the Center for Creative Leadership, a top-ranked, global, nonprofit provider of leadership development and a pioneer in the field of global leadership research. These six steps are:

1. Pay attention
2. Withhold judgment
3. Reflect
4. Clarify
5. Summarize
6. Share

PLEASE AND THANK YOU: STILL THE MAGIC WORDS

A review of the strategies and tools found in this book to advance your career makes it clear that some of them will take some practice or perhaps even years to master. Some of them will require the rewiring of deeply rooted habits or behaviors. But the simple habit of always using the words "please" and "thank you" is both easy and powerful.

In fact, the use of these "magic words" is something that I have observed is taught since childhood in many cultures. In American culture, the use of these simple words is found in episodes of children's TV shows like Barney & Friends, and there's even an entire book (*Please and Thank You Are Magic Words* by Amarinda Charles) dedicated to the subject.

So why is it so important to remember to consistently use please and thank you? Let's start with **please.** This word, like no other, denotes respect, because it tells the other party that, even if it is their job and responsibility (as a subordinate, a vendor, or a colleague) to do something for you, you are not using your position to mandate action. The use of "please" also lets others know that you have manners — something that, sadly, I have seen missing at all levels of organizations. Most importantly, the failure to ask for things nicely quickly tarnishes your professional image and starts to erode respect for you.

As for **thank you**, these two simple words demonstrate appreciation and gratitude. Most human beings thrive in environments where they are appreciated, and a simple "thank you" goes a long way to show that appreciation. Over my career, I have seen my fair share of employee engagement surveys, and lack of appreciation is one of the three things that come up as frequent grievances (the other two are poor work-life balance and lack of effective leadership). Expressing gratitude as part of your day-to-day communications enhances your image and strengthens your work relationships with peers, vendor partners, and your supervisor. Expressing gratitude is one of those things I have observed is well-received (and, in some cases, expected) across cultures and in all the countries where I have had the opportunity to work.

Lastly, be sure to extend the use of these two words to written communications. In fact, I could argue that using them in emails and formal written communications is even more important than using them verbally, because they leave a paper trail of how you treat others at work.

Here's a real-life example to support this point. A few jobs ago, one of my peers at the company where I worked had an executive assistant who, for some reason, did not like him. This dislike was unjustified and unfair, but we all know it happens. Her obsession with her boss reached a point where she actually filed a complaint with the company's human resources department about the way he treated her. The company's policy called for an investigation any time such a complaint was made and, as you would expect, the investigation included a review of written communications as a natural way to prove or disprove the validity of the claim. After reviewing dozens of emails, the company's HR department concluded that those communications, coupled with the testimony of others who actually vouched for my peer's professional demeanor, resulted in a quick dismissal of the complaint. The moral of this story is that consistent courteous written communications are important for more than good interpersonal relationships.

So please, always use the magic words. Thank you.

CHAPTER 7

THE INTERVIEW

Whether you are seeking your first job, going after the CEO role, or trying to land a great freelance gig, there will always be an interview along the road.

It is also a fact that, in many cases, the interview (or interviews)—much more than your qualifications and experience—is what determines whether you land the job or not. Therefore, effective and smart interviewing is a fundamental skill to acquire as you grow your career. In this chapter, we will review some practical strategies and tactics to help you nail the interview.

INTERVIEW PREP

Nothing improves your chances of landing a job more than showing up very well prepared for an interview. Unlike whatever goes on inside the company that's hiring, preparing for the interview is 100% under your control, so you would be remiss not to put the time and effort into this stage of the process.

When I was in San Francisco, I had an open role for a marketing channel manager, and the company recruiter found an amazing candidate that met or exceeded all of the requirements of the job. He also had a Berkeley plus Ivy League education. As is customary, we conducted a screening telephone call that he passed with flying colors. Next was the in-person interview at our offices on California street, in the heart of the San Francisco financial district.

The day of the interview arrived, and the job was really his to lose. When I asked him to tell me what he knew about the company, he simply said, "You guys are a bank, right?" From there on, it went further downhill. When I asked if he had any questions, he said, "Not really."

Naturally, we did not extend an offer to this candidate. My conclusion was that he simply had no interest in the role or the company, he already had another offer in the bag, and we were just his second or third option. But then, the following week, the recruiter told me that, when she let him know we would not be offering him the job, he was very disappointed, and he did not fully understand why. All the smarts, experience, and pedigreed education could not make up for the lack of preparation for the interview.

To make sure this does not happen to you, here are seven interview preparation best practices I've learned and applied to win jobs throughout my career.

1. Research the company.

Today, we have unprecedented access to a company's information, even if the firm is not publicly traded. In addition to the company's website, you can also "get the scoop" on your prospective employer from its social media channels (LinkedIn can be particularly helpful), its Wikipedia page, and the LinkedIn profiles of its top executives. In addition, and of particular interest to you as a candidate, is the company's Glassdoor reviews. Glassdoor is filled with employee reviews which provide invaluable insights into the company's culture and benefits, and even reviews of its CEO. If you are interviewing for a publicly traded company or a financial services institution, you can easily access its financial statements which provide a treasure trove of insights into the business performance of the institution over the course of time. All of this data will help you move the interview from a one-way interrogation session about you to a deep discussion about the company and how you can help it achieve its business objectives.

2. Research the interviewer.

With so much at stake during an interview, it is easy to fall into the trap that the conversation is all about you. Quite the opposite; the interview is about the needs of the employer and their need to determine if you are the person to help them "scratch the itch." And the person who has the biggest say on whether you are that person or not is the interviewer. It is therefore incumbent upon you to know as much as possible about the interviewer and use the interview to connect with them intellectually and emotionally. Here, once again, the good news is that, in the age of the internet, there is quite a bit of data about the person in front of you, even if they are "internet introverts." A simple Google search can reveal many things about a professional, above and beyond what you can gather from a review of their LinkedIn profile. The idea is to find out what makes the person "tick," what they are passionate about and, ideally, if you have something in common that you can casually bring up during the interview to establish a human connection. Perhaps it is a cause they care about, a passion about their alma mater, a hobby, or even a city where you both have lived. Even more powerful is knowing somebody in common, which in our increasingly connected world has become more likely than ever. Invest some time researching your interviewer so that, by the time you walk into the interview, you feel like you've already met them.

3. Research and "live" the role.

Normally, by the time you get to the interview, the recruiter has shared with you a job description or some type of similar document outlining the responsibilities and qualifications for the role. Be sure to read this document in detail more than once, looking for subtleties or keywords that can provide information about what the job is really like. This exercise is really important, but it is not enough. You are also well served to go online and read the job descriptions of the same role at other companies which can help you better understand and discuss the role in terms that complement the employer's own job description. Also, build a mental bridge between your current role and the one you are interviewing for so that you can talk about how they are similar. Your experience would allow you to "hit the ground running." Additionally, prepare by conducting a visualization exercise during which you see yourself doing the job: completing tasks, attending meetings, and contributing. As part of this exercise, imagine yourself very happy in the role and delighted that you came on board. All of these strategies will get you in a mind space that will allow you to discuss the role comfortably and authoritatively.

4. Prepare for behavioral questions.

Behavioral questions help the interviewer understand how you would act or react during certain situations in the workplace. They are normally framed as questions about how you reacted to, or handled, a difficult or uncomfortable situation that you faced in the past. A typical, and common, behavioral question is something along the lines of "tell me about a time when you had a disagreement with a coworker and how you managed." To help structure a response to behavioral questions, global leadership consulting company Development Dimensions International (DDI) developed the STAR interviewing method, which comprises:

- **ST: Situation/Task** - Explain the situation or task so others understand the context.

- **A: Action** - Give details about what you or another person did to handle the situation.

- **R: Result** - Describe what was achieved by the action and why it was effective.

This model makes it easy to structure your response to behavioral questions so that, when they arise, you already have a framework for responding. Equally important to effectively handling behavioral questions is to have a mental list of such likely questions beforehand, along with prepared responses for them. For example, assume that there will be at least one question about conflict. Have the specifics in your mind so that you don't have to improvise mid-interview, which is inherently risky. It is best to have a handful of these questions identified and rehearsed so that, when they are posed to you, you can simply respond in your best storytelling style.

Lastly, I advise against writing down answers to possible interview questions and using them as "cheat sheets" during an interview.

Referring to those notes mid-interview would look awkward and be difficult to pull off, even during an online video interview.

5. Add value from the get-go.

Certain professionals, lawyers, and therapists are notorious for ensuring that every minute of their time is billable. Their hard-earned knowledge is an invaluable asset, and it should not be given freely. In my personal experience, though, a job interview is a great time to give a little in order to receive a lot. This is a good time to provide the interviewer a preview of the value you would bring to the company by giving them a "teaser," and you can do this by acting as if you were already on the job. An optimal time to use this strategy is when you are given a chance to ask questions. Rather than asking mundane things like, "Can you tell me about the culture of the company," you can use this time to ask probing questions that you can then use to insert your point of view on how you would approach a real-life problem or opportunity. For example, you could ask the interviewer, "Can you please share with me the greatest challenge you have in the area of talent acquisition and retention?" After they tell you what that is (because every company has some sort of challenge in this area), you can follow up with how you faced a similar situation at a prior role and how you successfully tackled the problem. This approach, which is a behavioral question in reverse, can help the interviewer visualize you in the role.

6. Prepare for objections.

As it is often the case during a sales call (and an interview is, essentially, a type of sales call), there are times when an objection to your job candidacy may arise in the course of an interview. This is especially common when your profile may not be a 100% perfect fit against the job description. For example, let's say that you are interviewing for a very senior marketing role with a company that has a large advertising budget. You have managed moderate ad budgets before, but the interviewer may have reservations about your ability to manage the complexities associated with large media buys through multiple channels. The first step in overcoming this challenge is to identify likely objections beforehand and be prepared with simple, but decisive, responses to them. In our example, you would state that, although you have not managed massive ad budgets, the strategic thinking and ability to leverage analytics to optimize media performance is an infinitely scalable and transferable skill. Go through what you know about the role and ask yourself, objectively, if there are gaps that you, if you were the hiring manager, would identify in your profile. Be prepared to overcome each and every possible objection.

7. Have killer questions ready.

It has been my experience for decades that, many times, jobs are won or lost at the end of the interview when you are offered the opportunity to ask questions. This is the part of the interview where you are controlling the conversation, and you should not waste this time with "filler" questions, the answers to which you will find out if you are hired anyway. On the contrary, ask questions that focus on the business, its challenges, and opportunities so that the interview turns into a smart and strategic conversation between two professionals who, together, can take the company to the next level. For example, if the company's financials are publicly available, pick a key performance indicator, say revenue or net income, analyze its trend over the last few quarters or years, and ask why the number is trending one way or another. Such a question will send a message to your interviewer that you took the time to prepare, that you are analytical in nature, and that you understand the fundamentals of business—all of which are great things in a candidate. This will be far more effective than asking how many days of vacation the company offers, which is not only trivial but already signals where your true interests lie.

Here are the seven interview prep best practices, summarized for you:

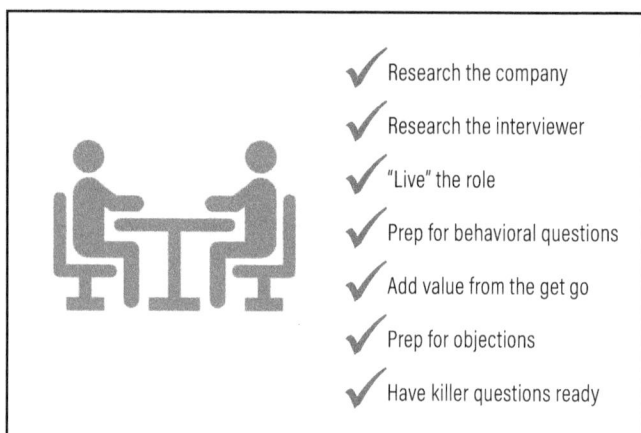

- ✔ Research the company
- ✔ Research the interviewer
- ✔ "Live" the role
- ✔ Prep for behavioral questions
- ✔ Add value from the get go
- ✔ Prep for objections
- ✔ Have killer questions ready

THE INTERVIEW BASICS

In addition to great preparation, there are three basics to successful interviews that you should bear in mind during these important events in your career.

1. Be on time.

Actually, don't be on time. Be very early, even if you have to wait in your car or in a lobby for twenty minutes. As somebody who has interviewed and hired dozens of people over three decades, I can tell you that, if you are late to my interview, even if you have the best excuse in the world, your chances of landing the job decrease by more than 80%. As some of my Japanese colleagues pointed out to me many times while I worked for Japan's largest financial institution, "If you are on time, you are late."

2. Look the part.

On interview day, be sure to dress in a way that projects professionalism, even if you know that is not how you will likely dress if you land the job. Years ago, I worked at a digital marketing agency with an extremely informal dress code (actually, there wasn't one), and I had the opportunity to interview with a very large financial institution headquartered in Charlotte, North Carolina. At that time, I did not own a single tie, let alone a business suit. But the opportunity was significant in so many ways. It could change the trajectory of our family if it were to materialize. My wife and I had young children and lots of expenses and, therefore, every penny counted. Buying a suit was, therefore, an agonizing decision. After all, if I did not get the job, the suit would be a terrible waste of money. Fortunately, my wife talked some sense into me and convinced me not to just get a nice suit, but to buy the absolute best suit I could afford. According to her calculations, the percentage of return on investment on such a purchase would be in the tens of thousands. So I went to a very high-end retailer and spent an unimaginable amount of money on a classic, fine Italian suit. The psychological impact of wearing these amazing garments took my confidence to another level, which must have shown during the interview. Not only did I have the brains to get the job done, but I belonged there, with high-powered, highly compensated executives. I got the job. So, please do look your absolute best on interview day.

3. Send a thank-you note.

You may be surprised that, in my experience, about one-third of all people I have interviewed do not send a post-interview thank-you note. This tells me that a significant percentage of job seekers out there do not understand this very fundamental step in the interview process. From the perspective of the hiring manager, not receiving this thank you note can only mean one of three things: a) the candidate is clueless, b) the candidate is not really interested in the job, or c) they forgot. None of these three reflect the traits of the person they want in the team. So, please make the post-interview thank-you note part of your routine. And, if you tend to forget these kinds of things, simply pre-write the email, let it sit on your outbox, and put a marker on your calendar to remind you to send it, ideally within twenty-four hours of the conclusion of the interview. Lastly, if you were interviewed by more than one person, please be sure that all interviewers receive a separate thank-you note.

VIDEO INTERVIEWS

Today, most screening, and even final, job interviews are conducted over video using platforms like Zoom or Microsoft Teams. While these remote interviews are great because you can do them from the comfort of your home, here are some important considerations and tips to help you nail this part of the hiring process:

- Test your equipment before a video interview. Ensure your camera, computer microphone, and speakers are all in working order. Use a laptop instead of a cell phone so that you'll look your best.

- Carefully consider your setting to ensure there's plenty of light and there are no distracting objects in the background. I once interviewed a candidate who happened to be a Las Vegas Raiders fan and had a huge Raiders flag as the backdrop of his home office, which was a huge distraction for me during the interview (and I'm a Raiders fan…!)

- Ensure that you are dressed appropriately for an interview. We all know that you are probably wearing shorts and flip flops, but you have to look professional from the waist up.

- Make sure you have full privacy and no distractions. Keep your pets away and ensure someone is taking care of the baby during the interview. Also, as best as you can, ensure that household noise, like the washing machine or your teenage kid's drum practice, is blocked.

- When the interview starts, look directly at your computer's camera, as this is the closest thing to direct eye contact during a video interview.

- Log into the call prior to the start of the interview — you don't want to find out that you have a non-working URL or can't connect when the interviewer is already online and waiting for you.

- Close all other applications and tabs on your computer so that you can give the interviewer your undivided attention.

ASKING FOR THE JOB

While attending Cal State L.A. as an undergraduate business student, I took a sales class as one of my program electives. One would think that a curriculum filled with finance, economics, and business calculus would be more appropriate for a business education. But it turns out that, to this day, I still remember and use some of the concepts from that class (incidentally, I cannot say the same about business calculus, which I barely passed…after two tries….).

In addition to some elementary things about sales, our professor emphasized the importance of Asking for the Sale. The concept was simply that, in any sales process, there comes a time when you simply have to manifest to your prospect that you want their business. Well, job-seeking, at its core, is a sales activity like any other, except you are the product. It follows then that, at some point in the hiring process, you have to Ask for the Sale by stating emphatically and in no uncertain terms that you want the job.

Asking for the job is important, because it sends two very important messages to the hiring manager: 1) you are indeed interested in the role and 2) you are clear, decisive, and transparent with your intentions. This second point tells your manager-to-be that, if they hire you, they can expect the kind of direct, simple communication that most companies want and need.

When do you ask for the job? Just like in the sales world, you may need to ask for the job on more than one occasion, starting at the end of the job interview, after you have asked your smart questions. This desire for the job can also be reinforced in your thank-you note and, if a recruiter or headhunter is involved in the hiring process, in follow-up or debriefing conversations with those individuals. So don't be shy. Ask for the job!

FOLLOW THROUGH

My second job out of college was in consumer finance as a loan officer for the now defunct Household Finance Corporation (HFC). I recall going to the interview with Greg the branch manager, a friendly and non-nonsense guy from the Midwest. The interview went well. He liked the fact that I spoke Spanish, because a large percentage of the branch's customer base (located in San Fernando, California) was Hispanic. Now, back in the day, there was no email. The only way to follow up with your interviewer was to either call, send a letter, or show up at the place of work.

I felt that it would be good to follow up and let Greg know that I really wanted the job, so I called the branch. It took me a few tries, but he finally came to the phone and, lo and behold, he told me that, if I wanted the job, I could start the following week.

This HFC branch was next to a blue-collar bar so, when we had a good sales day, several of us would go next door for a beer. On one occasion, Greg confessed to me that the real reason I got the job was because, in my post-interview actions, I demonstrated the behaviors he was looking for when he hired junior loan officers. He told me he wanted people who had follow through and persistence. To this day, when hiring somebody, I prefer candidates who, either directly or through the recruiter, manifest interest in the job beyond that initial post-interview thank-you note.

CHAPTER 8

USING YOUR UNIQUENESS TO YOUR ADVANTAGE

A key insight I have developed over three-plus decades of working around the world, and a key premise of this book, is that those things that we all assume work against us as we try to grow our careers are, in fact, our secret weapons and competitive advantages. We are going to explore that topic in some depth and, most importantly, discuss real-life, practical strategies built on this premise to help you grow your career.

THE DE&I REPRESENTATION DEMAND AND SUPPLY PARADIGM

In 1961, President John F. Kennedy signed Executive Order No.10925 which mandated that government contractors take affirmative action to ensure that "job applicants are employed without regard for their race, creed, color or national origin." That order was the genesis of the concept of affirmative action and one of the earliest references to these words. Today, of course, the term "affirmative action" is perceived as antiquated, and it is often associated with things like mandatory quotas.

In place of Affirmative Action, the government and the private sector have now moved to the concept of Diversity, Equity, and Inclusion (DE&I), which is now part of the human resources strategy of many organizations. Generally speaking, DE&I is the collection of strategies, policies, and tactics of an organization that are designed to promote the fair treatment and full participation of all employees and, in particular, those who belong to groups that, historically, have been underrepresented because of their identity or disability.

Regardless of your political and personal views on the subject, the fact remains that most large employers and many mid-sized ones have at least some resources and programs allocated to hiring, promoting, and retaining diverse employees. Some of these companies have made DE&I a priority because of societal, regulatory, or investor pressures, while others do so because their leaders honestly believe it is the right thing to do. Yet others do so because of a combination of these two. Regardless of the reason, what matters for this discussion is that the growing importance of DE&I within enterprises presents unique opportunities for prospective and incumbent employees that are part of underrepresented groups.

So, in practicality, what does the growing prominence of DE&I for employers mean to women and diverse professionals who are looking to advance their careers? The answer is simply that, whether employers believe in the altruism or the business case of a diverse workforce, they are under increased pressure to employ people across the entire spectrum of diversity. Today, this is generally true at all levels of the organization. What that means is that there are more opportunities than ever for women and people of color to occupy management roles (at all levels), C-level and executive jobs, and board-of-director positions.

Now, that does not mean that you, as a professional, will have access to these leadership roles just by being a woman or "diverse." In fact, some will argue that women and people of color need to perform at a higher level than their white male counterparts just to be considered for these opportunities. I have not personally experienced this and, therefore, do not have a strong point of view on this matter. What I do know is that, compared to just a few decades ago, the "rest of us" have an unprecedented number of opportunities to earn senior and executive leadership roles.

What is also a fact, though, is that women and minority underrepresentation in the C-suite and boardroom continues to be a reality in North America and Western Europe, so it seems there's much opportunity out there.

IMPROBABLE FACT #7

According to the Harvard Law School Forum on Corporate Governance and Russell Reynolds Associates, as of 2023, only 9% of CEOs in the S&P 100 were women. The traditional CEO feeder roles of CFO, COO, and P&L leaders show significant underrepresentation of women, which makes the path toward CEO that much more difficult.

So, assuming we agree that there's more opportunity than ever, how exactly can a professional from a diverse background take advantage of today's thinking about representation in the workforce?

In my experience, it all starts with an objective assessment of who we are as professionals and, specifically, as a woman or "diverse" professional. This is not about judging ourselves and asking if we are qualified, or ideal, for leadership and senior roles. Rather, it is about making a list of those things that are unique to us and can help fill a gap or improve something when we are placed in one of these senior roles.

Let's take a real-life example of a good friend of mine who is a Mexican-American woman with extensive experience in retail, but who had been stuck in regional retail operations at her company. For ten-plus years, she was a regional director overseeing approximately ten stores in southern California. When we met, she confided in me that, as grand as her "director" corporate title sounded, in reality, she was practically a regional manager seeing day-to-day operations in a limited footprint, with no opportunity to innovate or influence strategy for her employer. With much sacrifice, she completed her MBA in hopes that this new credential would position her for consideration for a better role, but this was all to no avail. She was stuck.

After a long conversation, we both quickly came to the conclusion that she needed a strategy to advance her career, or she would have to leave and find a more suitable role somewhere else. She told me that her preference would be to stay with her current employer. So she drafted a plan that, more or less, had these steps:

1. Review of her employer's business strategy.

She studied her organization's annual report, its investor calls, analysts' write-ups, and all-hands employee town hall meetings recordings to get a clear idea of the firm's challenges, opportunities, and strategic direction. This helped her understand if she had something that the organization needed. After doing this homework, my friend learned that a combination of market shifts and business opportunity pointed to an eventual expansion into certain communities of color, and more specifically, Hispanic communities.

2. An analysis of the leadership of the organization through the lens of diversity.

Her objective here was to identify pockets of misrepresentation. After conducting this analysis, it was obvious to my friend that her organization's executive team (CEO and direct reports) lacked diversity and did not reflect the makeup of the brand's customer base or the marketplace. After taking just these two steps, it became evident to her that there was real opportunity.

3. Research of the employer's current emphasis, prioritization and sense of urgency about DEI.

She then asked: How pressing was diverse representation for the organization? After inquiring here and there, my friend learned that the company's board of directors was growing increasingly worried about the optics (and potential investor and community backlash) of the homogeneity of the organization's executive team. It seemed that the pressure was growing more intense with every board meeting. The board, whether acting altruistically or not, wanted results in this area in the short term.

4. Résumé review.

As part of her plan, she then reviewed her résumé to objectively ascertain if she had the qualifications, experience, and executive presence needed to capitalize on an opportunity to join the executive team, should it present itself. This was a difficult exercise for her, because it required that she look at herself from the outside in, leaving aside any personal components of her story. The reality is that, as much as a person may feel that their professional and personal journey makes them deserving of a great career, organizations do not care much about that. It is about what she could do for the organization. Yes, she may have been the first person in her family to earn a college degree, which was indeed very meritorious, but it was trivial when it came to handing her an important part of a business. A hard look at her own résumé revealed that she was, in fact, qualified and ready for the next step up.

5. A plan of attack.

Now that she had established that there was a strong fit between the opportunity and her professional background, she put together a strong, well-timed, and deliberate plan to ensure that preparation met opportunity. In her case, the plan centered on creating new opportunities for exposure to the CEO, the board, and members of the executive team, along with an emphasis on enhancing her executive presence. Within six months, the CEO kicked off a reorganization, and she was asked to join the executive team as the company's new executive vice president.

In summary, diverse and women professionals should take full advantage of the social and business environment changes occurring in North America and Western Europe by making their "difference" a competitive advantage.

YOUR SECOND LANGUAGE IS YOUR SECRET WEAPON

There was a time in America, not too long ago, when immigrants from countries where English is not the primary language would discourage their children from learning or using their parents' mother tongue. This was because these parents wanted their children to be fully assimilated into American culture. The thinking went that, by erasing any traces of the parents' original culture and language, the child would be better off in school and beyond. This was common, for example, amongst Italian and Hispanic families.

Over the years, as I talked to second generation American professionals who were discouraged from inheriting their parents' native language, they often told the story with regret. They often shared with me that they wished their parents had done more to ensure that they retained their ancestral language now that they were professionals in an increasingly global economy.

The irony in all of this is, of course, is that many middle-class families will pay for their college-aged children to enroll in semester abroad programs in hopes that they will pick up a second language through an in-country immersive experience. I see this in some Hispanic families who will spend a fortune sending their children to Spain or Latin America for a term so that they can pick up some Spanish, when all that was needed was to push their young children to speak the language at the dinner table.

But if you are one of the ones that either immigrated into a new country with your mother tongue or had immigrant parents who insisted you speak their native language, you are in luck. The reason is simply because, as business becomes more global, speaking and writing a second language means that you have a competitive advantage in the job marketplace.

IMPROBABLE FACT #8

According to the U.S. Census Bureau, as of 2023, 21.6% of people in the United States speak a language other than English at home. That's one in every five adults.

Earlier in the book, I told my story about my very first international assignment, in Mexico City. That opportunity would have never presented itself unless I spoke (and wrote) in Spanish. In fact, and to be truthful, there were other analysts in my team that were better at the job than I, but all of their competence was for naught, because the job required proficiency in the language, ideally as a native speaker. That time, my second language eliminated all of my competition.

In some cases, a person may have grown up around a second language and was not encouraged to be fluent at it, but had enough exposure to it so that they can at least understand the basics. If this is your case, then the good news is that you have a head start in becoming professionally proficient in the language. Since your brain is already trained to understand the language and you have a vocabulary foundation, then all it may take is a combination of some formal training and consuming media in the language. Better yet, insert yourself in a social group that speaks the language, and you can have fun while you add to your professional credentials. This means that, with a combination of work and fun, you can pick up that coveted second language that can be just the differentiator you need to boost your career.

LEVERAGING AUTHENTICITY: HUMOR IN THE WORKPLACE

There was a time when women and people of color had to assume the behaviors, dress, and speech of white males in order to fit in and advance their careers. And, while I still see some of that today, my observation is that things have, indeed, changed. We now live in an era when professionals can bring their authentic selves to work.

Naturally, this is a great development from a societal point of view. However, this growing acceptance of who we are also comes with opportunities for advancing our careers because, in some cases, those things that are uniquely ours can also be the things that workplaces need from their best leaders.

Let me share a real-life example. Those who know people from the Caribbean (both Spanish- and English-speaking) can tell you that, culturally, there's a predisposition for humor, a good laugh, and a friendly smile. If you don't believe me, take a trip to Puerto Rico, Jamaica, or the Dominican Republic, and you will see a friendly smile is always just around the corner.

At the same time, we are now learning the importance of humor and levity in the workplace. For example, researchers Lehmann-Willenbrock and Allen (2014) observed the behavior of fifty-four teams in industrial organizations in Germany over two years by videotaping their team meetings. They found that humor in meetings triggered positive socio-emotional behaviors such as the active encouragement of participation and problem-solving behaviors. Further, humor patterns in meetings were positively related to team performance (e.g., reaching targets or self-reported team efficiency) both immediately and after two years.

This research supports my own experience which has taught me that, in workplaces where there's humor (of the right kind, of course), professionals tend to be more creative, supportive, and productive. If you happen to come from a background where laughter and humor is part of daily life, you can use that authentic part of yourself to positively influence the workplace, grow your influence, and advance your career.

One caveat: Another thing that has changed in the workplace is sensitivities to just about everything, which means that we all have to be extra careful with the type of humor that we bring to work. Be sure that you are not getting a laugh at the expense of others. Also, avoid making jokes that would insult your colleagues. That applies to self-deprecating humor, too. I once learned this the hard way when I showed up a few minutes late to a meeting and joked that it was ok because, as a Hispanic person, I am wired to be a few minutes late. The joke, which was clearly aimed at myself, bothered a person in the room who, after the meeting, made it clear to me that making fun of cultural stereotypes did not help other Hispanic people at the company. Point well taken, and lesson learned.

However, assuming that you are careful not to offend anybody, you should most certainly use humor, or any other trait that is part of who you are, to make a positive impact at work. This will help you advance your career.

ADVANTAGE, WOMEN

Over my career, I have observed time and again how many of my female colleagues seem to have the ability to understand something immediately, without the need for conscious reasoning. That, by definition, is called intuition. I am not saying males lack intuition. In fact, earlier in this book, I alluded to my development of this sixth sense due to growing up in adverse circumstances. This is different. My observation is that many women can sense nonverbal cues and social hints in business situations that I, for example, only see long after the fact.

Imagine having the ability to read the minds of everybody in a business meeting. Wouldn't that give you an immense advantage, save time, and enable you to contribute at another level? While heightened intuition is not quite mind reading, it is the next best thing.

One of my best friends from an earlier job in financial services once confided in me that she was able to "see through the bull," not just in meetings, but also in one-to-one conversations. She described it as her superpower and further shared that this superior instinct had allowed her to anticipate problems at work, understand who was really an ally and, most interestingly, to pick up on opportunities.

Entrepreneur and FinTech pioneer Heather R. Stone wrote an article in which she makes a compelling case for the concept that a woman's intuition plays a powerful role in effective leadership. Stone points to the fact that men's and women's brains are inherently different. For example, according to the author, research indicates that women enjoy enhanced activity in the brain's prefrontal cortex, which is the "emotional brain." The hypothesis then follows that a more developed emotional brain enables women to be more attuned to things like understanding their own feelings and sensing the emotions of others. Used the right way, this is a profound and immensely powerful tool in social and work situations.

In my own household, where I am the only male and I am surrounded by my wife and our daughters, this is a topic of constant debate. My wife asserts that women do have an advantage over males in the intuition department. She encourages our daughters to be aware of this gift and to fully leverage it in all aspects of their lives. I agree. This advice is in line with the main premise of this book, which is to take advantage of everything and anything that we have at our disposal to advance our career and grow as leaders.

Intuition, however, is just one way for women to use their unique qualities to advance in the workplace. Renowned life coach Susie Moore has captured six ways in which women can harness their skills without compromising their feminine qualities:

- **Own your feminine strengths.** According to Moore, multiple studies show that women are stronger listeners, better communicators, and more adept storytellers than men.

- **Share your own story.** Don't be afraid to reveal some vulnerability by sharing your story. Women who share their struggles generate empathy and respect as leaders.

- **Support other women.** Moore points to studies suggesting that the reason there is competition amongst women in the workplace is because there's a perceived limited number of management and C-level spots for women. However, she feels that women won't gain equality at work by keeping other women down.

- **Know your only competition is in the mirror.** She points out that men should not be perceived as the competition, let alone other women and constantly comparing yourself to others will only harm you. Seeing yourself as your own competition is key to your own progress and growth.

- **Be authentically yourself.** When Moore writes that "focusing on refining your natural gifts will do more for you than working on any weaker areas you have or trying to become someone you're not," she speaks the truth.

FINDING COMMON GROUND TO OVERCOME STEREOTYPES

Thus far, we have focused on tactics and strategies to help you advance your career. However, we should also address some of the challenges that women and people of color face in their professional daily lives and explore how we can turn uncomfortable situations into wins. I call this making lemonade out of lemons.

One major such challenge is the racial and gender stereotypes that have been pervasive and continue to persist in the workplace. Of particular difficulty is that these stereotypes are mostly negative and are rarely ever expressed openly. We also have to acknowledge that these stereotypes are not the exclusive domain of a certain gender, race, background, or sexual orientation. As a person of color, I can assure you that, for example, in the Hispanic community itself, these stereotypes are very much present. Sometimes, they run deep and are passed from generation to generation. When it comes to boxing people into stereotypes, many of us are guilty, even if that is hard for us to admit.

Now, in most work situations, these stereotypes and prejudices do not come to the surface. And since the legal and reputational risk related to discrimination is so high to companies, a lot of effort goes into training employees and setting policy to prevent employees from slipping up. Still, every now and then, and especially in social work situations, the occasional *faux pas* occurs. The good news is that, if you are on the receiving end of an inappropriate remark, you can choose to get offended and worked up about it, or you can use the situation to build a bridge, educate, and enhance your professional profile.

This has actually happened to me more than once. In one particular instance, the owner of a very large agricultural enterprise and I met during an after-work social event. When I introduced myself by my first name, my new friend proceeded to share with me that one of his Hispanic farm employees also went by my name. He was a good, loyal, hardworking worker and, despite his background, he had done well for himself, thanks to his boss's generosity. He went on and on about his employee, describing him as one would describe a good, loyal farm animal.

Because I have been exposed to these types of comments more than once, by now I can tell the true intention of these types of interactions. In this particular instance, I could unequivocally tell that my new friend had the best of intentions. He sincerely was simply trying to bond with me, and that was the first connection he came up with. This was him truly trying to find common ground without realizing that his story could be taken the wrong way by the person in front of him, who could well take exception to the implication that *all* Hispanics are the same. In my case, I take zero offense to a remark like that. In my mind, all work is honorable, and everybody's contributions are vital to a prosperous society, especially in an area like agriculture, which is the most vital of all industries.

This conversation then presented me with the opportunity to do two things: 1) Share some information about the rich diversity of Hispanics and the fact that people from Mexico to Argentina and from the Dominican Republic to Chile are all different. This simple lesson must, of course, be delivered without ridiculing or patronizing the other person. It is simply fact-sharing intended to educate. 2) Tell my own story as an immigrant as a proof point to dissipate whatever stereotypes the other person may have.

An exchange of this nature elevates your stature as a professional and helps build professional relationships based on mutual respect and good intentions. If you are ever in a situation where you are on the receiving end of a remark or conversation that does not feel right, take the high road and use the opportunity to educate the other person and find a true common ground.

PAYING IT BACK

ere is a fun exercise in gratitude. Think back to elementary school, and try to recall all the people who helped you along, starting perhaps with your kindergarten teacher or one of your grandparents. Then progress through middle school, and think about your siblings, parents, or maybe that sports coach who believed in you. Then move on to college or the equivalent, and on to your first job, and remember that one manager or peer who took you under their wing. Think about your spouse or partner, or maybe your pastor or rabbi. Oh, and even the workplace bully who, unbeknownst to him, was teaching you some important lessons about how to watch your back at work. And so on....

What this simple exercise will reveal is that dozens of people helped you along the way to where you are now. Most of them supported you selflessly, with no other intention than trying to help you grow and be better. All of these people helped you along the way with no coordination. They did this because they all understood, instinctively, that it is in our nature to help others. Helping others is one of the things that makes us human, and few things are as fulfilling and gratifying in life as making a positive impact on the lives of others.

As you watch your career blossom through your hard work, and perhaps by applying some of the strategies in this book, please be sure to pay it back by helping others along the way. You can do this by mentoring a young (or not-so-young) colleague at work. Or by taking some time every now and then and inviting a subordinate to your office to talk about their professional aspirations and giving them tips and ideas. Perhaps, one day, you can visit a high school with first-generation students to talk to them about your own professional journey. You can also look for that one LinkedIn contact who was just displaced, reach out, and offer to make some introductions and review their résumé.

This book is an attempt to do just that. If you got one single idea from it to help you use your uniqueness to grow your career, then please accept that as my way to pay back all those that have done so much for me, for so many years.

REFERENCES

References are listed in no particular order.

Kochhar, R. Parker K., Igielnik, R. (2022), *Majority of U.S. Workers Changing Jobs Are Seeing Real Wage Gains,* Pew Research Center.

Valentine, G. (2018), *Executive Presence: What Is It, Why You Need It and How to Get It,* Forbes Coaching Council.

Bradford, J. (2019), *Why Writing Ability Is the Most Important Skill in Business (And How to Acquire It)*, Forbes Agency Council.

Leading Effectively Staff (2023), *What Is Active Listening?,* Center for Creative Leadership.

Court, B. (2018), *What Is the STAR Format? Here's Your Complete Guide,* Development Dimensions International, Inc.

U.S. Department of Labor (1961), *Executive Order 10925,* Office of Federal Contract Compliance Programs.

Lieberman, G. Russell Reynolds Associates (2023), *Gender Diversity in the C-Suite,* Harvard Law School Forum on Corporate Governance.

Dietrich, S., Hernandez, E. (2022), *What Languages Do We Speak in the United States?*, United States Census Bureau.

Stone, H. (2021), *How Women's Intuition Plays a Powerful Role in Effective Leadership*, HeatherRStone.com.

Moore, S. (2017), *6 Ways to Successfully Play Up Your Feminine Strengths at Work,* susie-moore.com.

ACKNOWLEDGEMENTS

I would like to acknowledge the following people for their contributions to both my career and, subsequently, the creation of this book. First of all, my wife Angela Gonzalez for her unwavering support throughout the project.

Thank you, David Finkelstein, Alex Walterskirchen, Axel Clodi, Alex Aichner, Sergio Barrientos, and Matias Perel, for the opportunity to work alongside you to start companies; what a great learning experience and fun ride!

Thanks as well to Dr. Gloria A. Chance, the late Art Smith (the greatest brand marketer I've ever met), Dan Stevens, Mark Borrecco, and Isvara Wilson for believing in me and for your mentorship.

Last, but not the least, a million thanks to Stacey Miller for her invaluable contributions editing this book and to Steve Kuhn for the great design and layout work. You are all the best of the best!

ABOUT THE AUTHOR

Juan Silvera is a marketing, corporate communications and digital product strategy executive with more than thirty years real-life experience with some of the largest financial services firms in the world and marketing agency startups.

He has held Chief Marketing Officer positions at AgFirst Farm Credit Bank and Rabobank N.A., in addition to executive digital marketing roles at Wachovia / Wells Fargo, Bank of America and MUFG Union Bank. Prior to that, Juan was a principal in three digital marketing startups, two in the U.S. and one in Europe.

During his career he has lived and worked around the world in countries and cities from San Francisco, to Salzburg, Austria and from Charlotte to Mexico City, Miami, Utrecht, Netherlands and Caracas, Venezuela.

Juan is an alumnus from Cal State Los Angeles' School of Business and Economics and from Pepperdine University's Graziadio Business School, where he earned his MBA. He lives in Charlotte, North Carolina with his wife, Angela. They are proud parents of twin daughters, Andrea and Vanessa.

www.ingramcontent.com/pod-product-compliance
Lightning Source LLC
LaVergne TN
LVHW051419080426
835508LV00022B/3156